DEUTERONOMY

The Fifth Book of Moses

This WORKBOOK is designed to help assist the diligent study of those who would know the Word of God. It is written in a format that REQUIRES reading of the text from the Authorized King James Version of the Holy Scriptures.

The King James Bible correctly fills all of the available "blanks" in this workbook.

Other workbooks are available by contacting us:

By FAITH Publications
85 Hendersonville Hwy.
Walterboro, SC 29488

(843) 538-2269

www.faithbaptistchurch.us

DEUTERONOMY

Deut. 1:1-34:12 (KJV)

These be the words which _____ spake unto all Israel on this side Jordan in the wilderness, in the plain over against the Red sea, between Paran, and Tophel, and Laban, and Hazeroth, and Dizahab. [2] (There are _____ days' journey from Horeb by the way of mount Seir unto Kadesh-barnea.) [3] And it came to pass in the _____ year, in the _____ month, on the _____ day of the month, that Moses spake unto the children of Israel, according unto all that the Lord had given him in commandment unto them; [4] After he had slain Sihon the king of the Amorites, which dwelt in Heshbon, and Og the king of Bashan, which dwelt at Astaroth in Edrei: [5] On this side Jordan, in the land of _____ , began Moses to declare this law, saying, [6] The Lord our God spake unto us in Horeb, saying, Ye have _____ long _____ in this mount: [7] Turn you, and take your journey, and go to the mount of the Amorites, and unto all the places nigh thereunto, in the plain, in the hills, and in the vale, and in the south, and by the sea side, to the land of the Canaanites, and unto Lebanon, unto the great river, the river Euphrates. [8] Behold, I have set the _____ before you: _____ in and _____ the land which the Lord sware unto your fathers, Abraham, Isaac, and Jacob, to give unto them and to their seed after them.

[9] And I spake unto you at that time, saying, I am not able to _____ you myself _____ : [10] The Lord your God hath multiplied you, and, behold, ye are this day as the _____ of heaven for multitude. [11] (The Lord God of your fathers make you a thousand times so many more as ye are, and bless you, as he hath _____ you!) [12] How can I myself alone bear your cumbrance, and your burden, and your strife? [13] Take you wise men, and understanding, and known among your tribes, and I will make them rulers over you. [14] And ye answered me, and said, The thing which thou hast spoken is good for us to do. [15] So I took the chief of your tribes, wise men, and known, and made them heads over you, captains over thousands, and captains over hundreds, and captains over fifties, and captains over tens, and officers among your tribes. [16] And I charged your judges at that time, saying, Hear the _____ between your brethren, and judge _____ between every man and his brother, and the stranger that is with him. [17] Ye shall not _____ persons in judgment; but ye shall hear the _____ as well as the _____ ; ye shall not be _____ of the face of man; for the judgment is _____ : and the cause that is too hard for you, bring it unto me, and I will hear it. [18] And I commanded you at that time all the things which ye should do.

[19] And when we departed from Horeb, we went through all that great and terrible wilderness, which ye saw by the way of the mountain of the Amorites, as the Lord our God commanded us; and we came to Kadesh-barnea. [20] And I said unto you, Ye are come unto the mountain of the Amorites, which the Lord our God doth give unto us. [21] Behold, the Lord thy God hath set the land before thee: go up and _____ it, as the Lord God of thy fathers hath said unto thee; fear not, neither be discouraged.

[22] And ye came near unto me every one of you, and said, We will send men before us, and they shall search us out the land, and bring us word again by what _____ we must go up, and into what cities we shall come. [23] and the saying pleased me well: and I took _____ men of you, one of a tribe: [24] And they turned and went up into the mountain, and came unto the valley of Eshcol, and searched it out. [25] And they took of the fruit of the land in their hands, and brought it down unto us, and brought us word

DEUTERONOMY

again, and said, It is a _____ land which the Lord our God doth give us. [26] Notwithstanding ye would not go up, but _____ against the commandment of the Lord your God: [27] And ye _____ in your _____ , and said, Because the Lord hated us, he hath brought us forth out of the land of Egypt, to deliver us into the hand of the Amorites, to destroy us. [28] Whither shall we go up? our _____ have _____ our heart, saying, The people is greater and taller than we; the cities are great and walled up to heaven; and moreover we have seen the sons of the Anakims there. [29] Then I said unto you, Dread not, neither be _____ of them. [30] The Lord your God which goeth before you, he shall fight for you, according to all that he did for you in Egypt before your eyes; [31] And in the wilderness, where thou hast seen how that the Lord thy God bare thee, as a man doth bear his son, in all the way that ye went, until ye came into this place. [32] Yet in this thing ye did _____ believe the Lord your God, [33] Who went in the way before you, to search you out a place to pitch your tents in, in fire by night, to shew you by what way ye should go, and in a cloud by day. [34] And the Lord heard the voice of your _____ , and was wroth, and sware, saying, [35] Surely there shall not one of these men of this evil generation see that good land, which I sware to give unto your fathers, [36] Save _____ the son of Jephunneh; he shall see it, and to him will I give the land that he hath trodden upon, and to his children, because he hath wholly followed the Lord. [37] Also the Lord was angry with me for your sakes, saying, Thou also shalt not go in thither. [38] But _____ the son of Nun, which standeth before thee, he shall go in thither: _____ him: for he shall cause Israel to inherit it. [39] Moreover your little ones, which ye said should be a prey, and your children, which in that day had no knowledge between good and evil, they shall go in thither, and unto them will I give it, and they shall possess it. [40] But as for you, turn you, and take your journey into the _____ by the way of the Red sea. [41] Then ye answered and said unto me, We have _____ against the Lord, we will go up and fight, according to all that the Lord our God commanded us. And when ye had girded on every man his weapons of war, ye were ready to go up into the hill. [42] And the Lord said unto me, Say unto them, Go not up, neither fight; for I am _____ among you; lest ye be smitten before your enemies. [43] So I spake unto you; and ye would not hear, but rebelled against the commandment of the Lord, and went _____ up into the hill. [44] And the Amorites, which dwelt in that mountain, came out against you, and chased you, as bees do, and _____ you in Seir, even unto Hormah. [45] And ye returned and wept before the Lord; but the Lord would not hearken to your voice, nor give ear unto you. [46] So ye abode in _____ many days, according unto the days that ye abode there.

[2:1] Then we turned, and took our journey into the wilderness by the way of the Red sea, as the Lord spake unto me: and we compassed mount Seir many days. [2] And the Lord spake unto me, saying, [3] Ye have compassed this mountain long enough: turn you northward. [4] And command thou the people, saying, Ye are to pass through the coast of your brethren the children of _____ , which dwell in Seir; and they shall be _____ of you: take ye good heed unto yourselves therefore: [5] _____ not with them; for I will not give you of their _____ , no, not so much as a footbreadth; because I have given mount Seir unto _____ for a possession. [6] Ye shall buy meat of them for money, that ye may eat; and ye shall also buy water of them for money, that ye may drink. [7] For the Lord thy God hath _____ thee in all the works of thy

DEUTERONOMY

hand: he _____ thy walking through this great wilderness: these forty years the Lord thy God hath been _____ thee; thou hast lacked _____ . [8] And when we passed by from our brethren the children of Esau, which dwelt in Seir, through the way of the plain from Elath, and from Ezion-gaber, we turned and passed by the way of the wilderness of Moab. [9] And the Lord said unto me, Distress not the Moabites, neither contend with them in battle: for I will not give thee of their land for a _____ ; because I have given Ar unto the children of _____ for a possession. [10] The Emims dwelt therein in times past, a people great, and many, and tall, as the Anakims; [11] Which also were accounted _____ , as the Anakims; but the Moabites call them Emims. [12] The Horims also dwelt in Seir beforetime; but the children of Esau succeeded them, when they had destroyed them from before them, and dwelt in their stead; as Israel did unto the land of his possession, which the Lord gave unto them. [13] Now rise up, said I, and get you over the brook Zered. And we went over the brook Zered. [14] And the space in which we came from _____-_____ , until we were come over the brook Zered, was _____ and _____ years; until all the generation of the _____ of war were _____ out from among the host, as the Lord sware unto them. [15] For indeed the hand of the Lord was _____ them, to destroy them from among the host, until they were _____ .

[16] So it came to pass, when all the men of war were consumed and dead from among the people, [17] That the Lord spake unto me, saying, [18] Thou art to pass over through Ar, the coast of Moab, this day: [19] And when thou comest nigh over against the children of Ammon, distress them not, nor meddle with them: for I will not give thee of the land of the children of _____ any possession; because I have given it unto the children of _____ for a possession. [20] (That also was accounted a land of giants: giants dwelt therein in old time; and the Ammonites call them Zamzummims; [21] A people great, and many, and tall, as the Anakims; but the Lord _____ them before them; and they succeeded them, and dwelt in their stead: [22] As he did to the children of _____ , which dwelt in Seir, when he destroyed the Horims from before them; and they succeeded them, and dwelt in their stead even unto this day: [23] And the Avims which dwelt in Hazerim, even unto Azzah, the Caphtorims, which came forth out of Caphtor, destroyed them, and dwelt in their stead.)

[24] Rise ye up, take your journey, and pass over the river Arnon: behold, I have given into thine hand _____ the Amorite, king of Heshbon, and his land: begin to possess it, and contend with him in battle. [25] This day will I begin to put the _____ of thee and the _____ of thee upon the nations that are under the whole heaven, who shall hear report of thee, and shall tremble, and be in anguish because of thee.

[26] And I sent messengers out of the wilderness of Kedemoth unto Sihon king of Heshbon with words of peace, saying, [27] Let me pass through thy land: I will go along by the high way, I will neither turn unto the right hand nor to the left. [28] Thou shalt sell me meat for money, that I may eat; and give me water for money, that I may drink: only I will pass through on my feet; [29] (As the children of Esau which dwell in Seir, and the Moabites which dwell in Ar, did unto me;) until I shall pass over _____ into the land which the Lord our God giveth us. [30] But Sihon king of Heshbon would not let us pass by him: for the Lord thy God hardened his _____ , and made his _____ obstinate, that he might deliver him into thy hand, as appeareth this day. [31] And the Lord said unto me, Behold, I have begun to give Sihon and his land before thee:

DEUTERONOMY

_____ to _____ , that thou mayest inherit his land. [32] Then Sihon came out against us, he and all his people, to fight at Jahaz. [33] And the Lord our God delivered him before us; and we smote him, and his sons, and all his people. [34] And we took all his cities at that time, and utterly destroyed the men, and the women, and the little ones, of every city, we left none to remain: [35] Only the cattle we took for a prey unto ourselves, and the spoil of the cities which we took. [36] From Aroer, which is by the brink of the river of Arnon, and from the city that is by the river, even unto Gilead, there was not one city too strong for us: the Lord our God delivered all unto us: [37] Only unto the land of the children of Ammon thou camest not, nor unto any place of the river Jabbok, nor unto the cities in the mountains, nor unto whatsoever the Lord our God forbad us.

[3:1] Then we turned, and went up the way to Bashan: and _____ the king of _____ came out against us, he and all his people, to battle at Edrei. [2] And the Lord said unto me, _____ him _____ : for I will deliver him, and all his people, and his land, into thy hand; and thou shalt do unto him as thou didst unto Sihon king of the Amorites, which dwelt at Heshbon. [3] So the Lord our God _____ into our hands Og also, the king of Bashan, and all his people: and we smote him until none was left to him remaining. [4] And we took all his cities at that time, there was not a city which we took not from them, threescore cities, all the region of Argob, the kingdom of Og in Bashan. [5] All these cities were fenced with high walls, gates, and bars; beside unwalled towns a great many. [6] And we utterly destroyed them, as we did unto Sihon king of Heshbon, utterly destroying the men, women, and children, of every city. [7] But all the cattle, and the spoil of the cities, we took for a prey to ourselves. [8] And we took at that time out of the hand of the two kings of the Amorites the land that was on this side Jordan, from the river of Arnon unto mount Hermon; [9] (Which Hermon the Sidonians call Sirion; and the Amorites call it Shenir;) [10] All the cities of the plain, and all Gilead, and all Bashan, unto Salchah and Edrei, cities of the kingdom of Og in Bashan. [11] For only _____ king of Bashan remained of the remnant of _____ ; behold, his _____ was a bedstead of _____ ; is it not in Rabbath of the children of Ammon? _____ cubits was the length thereof, and _____ cubits the breadth of it, after the cubit of a man. [12] And this land, which we possessed at that time, from Aroer, which is by the river Arnon, and half mount Gilead, and the cities thereof, gave I unto the Reubenites and to the Gadites. [13] And the rest of _____ , and all _____ , being the kingdom of Og, gave I unto the _____ tribe of _____ ; all the region of Argob, with all Bashan, which was called the land of giants. [14] Jair the son of Manasseh took all the country of Argob unto the coasts of Geshuri and Maachathi; and called them after his own name, Bashan-havoth-jair, unto this day. [15] And I gave Gilead unto Machir. [16] And unto the _____ and unto the _____ I gave from _____ even unto the river Arnon _____ the valley, and the border even unto the river Jabbok, which is the border of the children of Ammon; [17] The plain also, and _____ , and the coast thereof, from _____ even unto the sea of the plain, even the _____ sea, under Ashdoth-pisgah eastward.

[18] And I commanded you at that time, saying, The Lord your God hath given you this land to possess it: ye shall pass over armed before your brethren the children of Israel, all that are meet for the war. [19] But your wives, and your little ones, and your cattle, (for I know that ye have much cattle,) shall abide in your cities which I have given

DEUTERONOMY

you; [20] Until the Lord have given rest unto your brethren, as well as unto you, and until they also possess the land which the Lord your God hath given them beyond Jordan: and then shall ye return every man unto his possession, which I have given you.

[21] And I commanded Joshua at that time, saying, Thine eyes have _____ all that the Lord your God hath done unto these two kings: so shall the Lord do unto all the kingdoms whither thou passest. [22] Ye shall not _____ them: for the _____ your _____ he shall _____ for you. [23] And I besought the Lord at that time, saying, [24] O Lord God, thou hast begun to shew thy servant thy greatness, and thy mighty hand: for what God is there in heaven or in earth, that can do according to thy works, and according to thy might? [25] I pray thee, let _____ go _____ , and _____ the good _____ that is beyond Jordan, that goodly mountain, and Lebanon. [26] But the Lord was _____ with me for your sakes, and would _____ hear me: and the Lord said unto me, Let it suffice thee; _____ no _____ unto me of this matter. [27] Get thee up into the top of _____ , and lift up thine _____ westward, and northward, and southward, and eastward, and _____ it with thine eyes: for thou shalt _____ go over this Jordan. [28] But charge _____ , and _____ him, and _____ him: for he _____ go over before this people, and he shall cause them to inherit the land which thou shalt see. [29] So we abode in the valley over against Beth-peor.

[4:1] Now therefore hearken, O Israel, unto the statutes and unto the judgments, which I teach you, for to do them, that ye may live, and go in and possess the land which the Lord God of your fathers giveth you. [2] Ye shall not _____ unto the word which I command you, neither shall ye _____ ought from it, that ye may _____ the _____ of the Lord your God which I command you. [3] Your eyes have seen what the Lord did because of Baal-peor: for all the men that followed Baal-peor, the Lord thy God hath destroyed them from among you. [4] But ye that did _____ unto the Lord your God are alive every one of you this day. [5] Behold, I have taught you statutes and judgments, even as the Lord my God commanded me, that ye should do so in the land whither ye go to possess it. [6] Keep therefore and do them; for this is your _____ and your _____ in the sight of the nations, which shall hear all these statutes, and say, Surely this great nation is a wise and understanding people. [7] For what nation is there so great, who hath God so nigh unto them, as the Lord our God is in all things that we call upon him for? [8] And what nation is there so great, that hath statutes and judgments so righteous as all this _____ , which I set before you this day? [9] Only take _____ to _____ , and keep thy soul _____ , lest thou _____ the things which thine eyes have seen, and lest they depart from thy heart all the days of thy life: but teach them thy sons, and thy sons' sons; [10] Specially the day that thou stoodest before the Lord thy God in Horeb, when the Lord said unto me, Gather me the people together, and I will make them hear my words, that they may _____ to fear me all the days that they shall live upon the earth, and that they may _____ their _____ . [11] And ye came near and stood under the mountain; and the mountain burned with fire unto the midst of heaven, with darkness, clouds, and thick darkness. [12] And the Lord spake unto you out of the midst of the fire: ye heard the voice of the words, but saw no similitude; only ye heard a voice. [13] And he declared unto you his covenant, which he commanded you to perform, even _____ commandments; and he wrote them upon two tables of _____ .

DEUTERONOMY

[14] And the Lord commanded me at that time to teach you statutes and judgments, that ye might do them in the land whither ye go over to possess it. [15] Take ye therefore good heed unto yourselves; for ye saw no manner of similitude on the day that the Lord spake unto you in Horeb out of the midst of the fire: [16] Lest ye _____ yourselves, and make you a graven image, the similitude of any figure, the likeness of male or female, [17] The likeness of any beast that is on the earth, the likeness of any winged fowl that flieth in the air, [18] The likeness of any thing that creepeth on the ground, the likeness of any fish that is in the waters beneath the earth: [19] And lest thou lift up thine eyes unto heaven, and when thou seest the sun, and the moon, and the stars, even all the host of heaven, shouldest be driven to _____ them, and _____ them, which the Lord thy God hath divided unto all nations under the whole heaven. [20] But the _____ hath taken you, and brought you forth out of the iron _____ , even out of Egypt, to be unto him a people of inheritance, as ye are this day. [21] Furthermore the Lord was angry with me for your sakes, and sware that I should not go over Jordan, and that I should not go in unto that good land, which the Lord thy God giveth thee for an inheritance: [22] But I must die in this land, I must not go over Jordan: but ye shall go over, and possess that good land. [23] Take heed unto yourselves, lest ye _____ the covenant of the Lord your God, which he made with you, and make you a graven image, or the likeness of any thing, which the Lord thy God hath forbidden thee. [24] For the Lord thy God is a consuming _____ , even a _____ God.

[25] When thou shalt beget children, and children's children, and ye shall have remained long in the land, and shall corrupt yourselves, and make a graven image, or the likeness of any thing, and shall do evil in the sight of the Lord thy God, to provoke him to anger: [26] I call _____ and _____ to _____ against you this day, that ye shall soon utterly perish from off the land whereunto ye go over Jordan to possess it; ye shall not prolong your days upon it, but shall utterly be destroyed. [27] And the _____ shall _____ you among the _____ , and ye shall be left _____ in number among the heathen, whither the Lord shall lead you. [28] And there ye shall serve gods, the work of men's hands, wood and stone, which neither see, nor hear, nor eat, nor smell. [29] But if from thence thou shalt _____ the Lord thy God, thou shalt _____ him, if thou _____ him with _____ thy _____ and with _____ thy _____ . [30] When thou art in tribulation, and all these things are come upon thee, even in the latter days, if thou turn to the Lord thy God, and shalt be _____ unto his voice; [31] (For the Lord thy God is a merciful God;) he will _____ forsake thee, neither destroy thee, nor forget the covenant of thy fathers which he sware unto them. [32] For ask now of the days that are past, which were before thee, since the day that God created man upon the earth, and ask from the one side of heaven unto the other, whether there hath been any such thing as this great thing is, or hath been heard like it? [33] Did ever _____ hear the _____ of God speaking out of the midst of the fire, as thou hast heard, and live? [34] Or hath God assayed to go and take him a nation from the midst of another nation, by temptations, by signs, and by wonders, and by war, and by a mighty hand, and by a stretched out arm, and by great terrors, according to all that the Lord your God did for you in Egypt before your eyes? [35] Unto _____ it was shewed, that thou mightest know that the _____ he is God; there is _____ else beside _____ . [36] Out of heaven he made thee to hear his voice, that he might instruct thee: and upon earth

DEUTERONOMY

he shewed thee his great fire; and thou heardest his words out of the midst of the fire. [37] And because he _____ thy fathers, therefore he _____ their seed after them, and brought thee out in his sight with his mighty power out of Egypt; [38] To drive out nations from before thee greater and mightier than thou art, to bring thee in, to give thee their land for an inheritance, as it is this day. [39] Know therefore this day, and consider it in thine heart, that the _____ he is _____ in _____ above, and upon the _____ beneath: there is none else. [40] Thou shalt keep therefore his statutes, and his commandments, which I command thee this day, that it may go well with thee, and with thy _____ after thee, and that thou mayest _____ thy _____ upon the earth, which the Lord thy God giveth thee, for ever.

[41] Then Moses severed _____ cities on this side Jordan toward the sunrising; [42] That the slayer might flee thither, which should kill his neighbour _____ , and hated him not in times past; and that fleeing unto one of these cities he might live: [43] Namely, _____ in the wilderness, in the plain country, of the _____ ; and _____ in _____ , of the _____ ; and _____ in _____ , of the _____ .

[44] And this is the _____ which Moses set before the children of Israel: [45] These are the _____ , and the _____ , and the _____ , which Moses spake unto the children of Israel, after they came forth out of Egypt, [46] On this side Jordan, in the valley over against Beth-peor, in the land of Sihon king of the Amorites, who dwelt at Heshbon, whom Moses and the children of Israel smote, after they were come forth out of Egypt: [47] And they possessed his land, and the land of Og king of Bashan, two kings of the Amorites, which were on this side Jordan toward the sunrising; [48] From Aroer, which is by the bank of the river Arnon, even unto mount Sion, which is Hermon, [49] And all the plain on this side Jordan eastward, even unto the sea of the plain, under the springs of Pisgah.

[5:1] And Moses called all Israel, and said unto them, Hear, O Israel, the statutes and judgments which I speak in your ears this day, that ye may _____ them, and _____ , and _____ them. [2] The _____ our God made a _____ with us in Horeb. [3] The Lord made not this covenant with our fathers, but with us, even us, who are all of us here alive this day. [4] The Lord talked with you face to face in the mount out of the midst of the fire, [5] (I stood between the Lord and you at that time, to shew you the word of the Lord: for ye were afraid by reason of the fire, and went not up into the mount;) saying,

[6] I am the Lord thy God, which brought thee out of the land of Egypt, from the house of bondage. [7] Thou shalt have none other _____ before me. [8] Thou shalt _____ make thee any graven _____ , or any _____ of any thing that is in _____ above, or that is in the _____ beneath, or that is in the _____ beneath the earth: [9] Thou shalt not _____ down thyself unto them, nor _____ them: for I the Lord thy God am a _____ God, visiting the _____ of the fathers upon the children unto the _____ and _____ generation of them that hate me, [10] And shewing _____ unto _____ of them that _____ me and _____ my commandments. [11] Thou shalt not take the _____ of the Lord thy God in _____ : for the Lord will not hold him _____ that taketh his name in vain. [12] _____ the _____ day to _____ it, as the Lord thy God hath commanded thee. [13] _____ days thou

DEUTERONOMY

shalt labour, and do all thy _____ : [14] But the _____ day is the _____ of the Lord thy God: in it thou shalt not do any _____ , thou, nor thy son, nor thy daughter, nor thy manservant, nor thy maidservant, nor thine ox, nor thine ass, nor any of thy cattle, nor thy stranger that is within thy gates; that thy manservant and thy maidservant may rest as well as thou. [15] And remember that thou wast a servant in the land of Egypt, and that the Lord thy God brought thee out thence through a _____ hand and by a _____ out arm: therefore the Lord thy God commanded thee to _____ the sabbath day.

[16] _____ thy father and thy mother, as the Lord thy God hath commanded thee; that thy days may be prolonged, and that it may go well with thee, in the land which the Lord thy God giveth thee. [17] Thou shalt not _____ . [18] Neither shalt thou commit _____ . [19] Neither shalt thou _____ . [20] Neither shalt thou _____ false _____ against thy neighbour. [21] Neither shalt thou _____ thy neighbour's _____ , neither shalt thou _____ thy neighbour's _____ , his _____ , or his _____ , or his _____ , his _____ , or his _____ , or _____ thing that is thy neighbour's.

[22] These words the Lord spake unto all your assembly in the mount out of the midst of the fire, of the cloud, and of the thick darkness, with a great voice: and he added _____ more. And he wrote them in _____ tables of stone, and delivered them unto me. [23] And it came to pass, when ye heard the voice out of the midst of the darkness, (for the mountain did burn with fire,) that ye came near unto me, even all the heads of your tribes, and your elders; [24] And ye said, Behold, the Lord our God hath shewed us his _____ and his greatness, and we have heard his voice out of the midst of the fire: we have seen this day that God doth talk with man, and he liveth. [25] Now therefore why should we die? for this great fire will consume us: if we hear the voice of the Lord our God any more, then we shall die. [26] For who is there of all flesh, that hath heard the voice of the living God speaking out of the midst of the fire, as we have, and lived? [27] Go thou near, and hear all that the Lord our God shall say: and speak thou unto us all that the Lord our God shall speak unto thee; and we will hear it, and do it. [28] And the Lord heard the voice of your words, when ye spake unto me; and the Lord said unto me, I have heard the voice of the words of this people, which they have spoken unto thee: they have well said all that they have spoken. [29] O that there were such an _____ in them, that they would _____ me, and _____ all my _____ always, that it might be _____ with them, and with their _____ for ever! [30] Go say to them, Get you into your tents again. [31] But as for thee, _____ thou here by me, and I will speak unto thee all the commandments, and the statutes, and the judgments, which thou shalt _____ them, that they may _____ them in the land which I give them to possess it. [32] Ye shall _____ to do therefore as the Lord your God hath commanded you: ye shall _____ turn aside to the _____ hand or to the _____ . [33] Ye shall _____ in _____ the ways which the Lord your God hath _____ you, that ye may _____ , and that it may be _____ with you, and that ye may _____ your days in the land which ye shall possess.

[6:1] Now these are the _____ , the statutes, and the judgments, which the Lord your God commanded to _____ you, that ye might do them in the land whither ye go to possess it: [2] That thou mightest _____ the Lord thy God, to _____ all

DEUTERONOMY

his statutes and his commandments, which I command thee, thou, and thy son, and thy son's son, all the days of thy life; and that thy days may be prolonged.

[3] Hear therefore, O Israel, and observe to _____ it; that it may be _____ with thee, and that ye may _____ mightily, as the Lord God of thy fathers hath _____ thee, in the land that floweth with milk and honey. [4] _____, O _____: The Lord our _____ is _____ Lord: [5] And thou shalt _____ the Lord thy God with _____ thine _____, and with _____ thy _____, and with all thy _____. [6] And these _____, which I command thee this day, shall be _____ thine _____: [7] And thou shalt _____ them _____ unto thy _____, and shalt _____ of them when thou _____ in thine _____, and when thou _____ by the _____, and when thou _____ _____, and when thou _____ up. [8] And thou shalt _____ them for a _____ upon thine _____, and they shall be _____ frontlets between thine _____. [9] And thou shalt _____ them upon the _____ of thy _____, and on thy _____. [10] And it shall be, when the Lord thy God shall have brought thee into the land which he sware unto thy fathers, to Abraham, to Isaac, and to Jacob, to _____ thee great and goodly cities, which thou _____ not, [11] And houses full of all _____ things, which thou _____ not, and wells digged, which thou _____ not, vineyards and olive trees, which thou _____ not; when thou shalt have eaten and be full; [12] Then _____ lest thou _____ the Lord, which brought thee forth out of the land of Egypt, from the house of _____. [13] Thou shalt _____ the Lord thy God, and _____ him, and shalt swear by his name. [14] Ye shall _____ go after other _____, of the gods of the people which are round about you; [15] (For the Lord thy God is a _____ God among you) lest the anger of the Lord thy God be kindled against thee, and destroy thee from off the face of the earth.

[16] Ye shall not _____ the Lord your God, as ye tempted him in Massah. [17] Ye shall _____ keep the commandments of the Lord your God, and his testimonies, and his statutes, which he hath commanded thee. [18] And thou shalt _____ that which is _____ and _____ in the _____ of the _____: that it may be well with thee, and that thou mayest go in and possess the good land which the Lord sware unto thy fathers, [19] To cast out all thine enemies from before thee, as the Lord hath spoken. [20] And when thy son _____ thee in time to come, saying, What mean the _____, and the _____, and the _____, which the Lord our God hath commanded you? [21] Then _____ shalt _____ unto thy son, We _____ Pharaoh's _____ in _____; and the _____ brought us _____ of Egypt with a _____ hand: [22] And the _____ shewed signs and wonders, great and sore, upon Egypt, upon Pharaoh, and upon all his household, before our eyes: [23] And he _____ us _____ from thence, that he might _____ us _____, to _____ us the _____ which he sware unto our fathers. [24] And the Lord commanded us to _____ all these statutes, to fear the Lord our God, for our _____ always, that he might _____ us alive, as it is at this day. [25] And it shall be our _____, if we observe to do all these commandments before the Lord our God, as he hath commanded us.

[7:1] When the Lord thy God shall bring thee into the land whither thou goest to _____ it, and hath cast out many nations before thee, the Hittites, and the

DEUTERONOMY

Girgashites, and the Amorites, and the Canaanites, and the Perizzites, and the Hivites, and the Jebusites, _____ nations _____ and _____ than thou; [2] And when the Lord thy God shall _____ them before thee; thou shalt smite them, and utterly _____ them; thou shalt make no _____ with them, nor shew _____ unto them: [3] Neither shalt thou make _____ with them; thy daughter thou shalt _____ give unto his son, nor his _____ shalt thou take unto thy son. [4] For they will _____ away thy son from _____ me, that they may serve other _____ : so will the anger of the Lord be kindled against you, and destroy thee suddenly. [5] But thus shall ye deal with them; ye shall _____ their _____ , and _____ down their _____ , and _____ down their _____ , and _____ their graven _____ with fire. [6] For thou art an holy people unto the Lord thy God: the Lord thy God hath chosen thee to be a special people unto himself, above all people that are upon the face of the earth. [7] The Lord did not set his love upon you, nor choose you, because ye were more in number than any people; for ye were the fewest of all people: [8] But _____ the Lord _____ you, and because he would _____ the _____ which he had sworn unto your fathers, hath the Lord brought you out with a mighty hand, and redeemed you out of the house of bondmen, from the hand of Pharaoh king of Egypt. [9] Know therefore that the Lord thy God, he is God, the _____ God, which keepeth covenant and mercy with them that love him and keep his commandments to a _____ generations; [10] And repayeth them that hate him to their face, to destroy them: he will not be slack to him that hateth him, he will repay him to his face. [11] Thou shalt therefore keep the commandments, and the statutes, and the judgments, which I command thee this day, to do them.

    [12] Wherefore it shall come to pass, if ye hearken to these judgments, and keep, and do them, that the Lord thy God shall keep unto thee the covenant and the mercy which he sware unto thy fathers: [13] And he will _____ thee, and _____ thee, and _____ thee: he will also bless the _____ of thy _____ , and the fruit of thy _____ , thy corn, and thy wine, and thine oil, the increase of thy kine, and the flocks of thy sheep, in the land which he sware unto thy fathers to give thee. [14] Thou shalt be _____ above _____ people: there shall not be male or female barren among you, or among your cattle. [15] And the Lord will take away from thee all sickness, and will put none of the evil diseases of Egypt, which thou knowest, upon thee; but will lay them upon all them that hate thee. [16] And thou shalt consume all the people which the Lord thy God shall deliver thee; thine eye shall have no pity upon them: neither shalt thou _____ their _____ ; for that will be a _____ unto thee. [17] If thou shalt say in thine heart, These nations are more than I; how can I dispossess them? [18] Thou shalt not be afraid of them: but shalt well _____ what the Lord thy God did unto Pharaoh, and unto all Egypt; [19] The great temptations which thine eyes saw, and the signs, and the wonders, and the mighty hand, and the stretched out arm, whereby the Lord thy God brought thee out: so shall the Lord thy God do unto all the people of whom thou art afraid. [20] Moreover the Lord thy God will send the _____ among them, until they that are left, and hide themselves from thee, be destroyed. [21] Thou shalt not be affrighted at them: for the _____ thy God is _____ you, a _____ God and _____ . [22] And the Lord thy God will put out those nations before thee by little and little: thou mayest not consume them at once, lest the

DEUTERONOMY

_____ of the field _____ upon thee. [23] But the Lord thy God shall _____ them unto thee, and shall destroy them with a mighty destruction, until they be destroyed. [24] And he shall deliver their kings into thine hand, and thou shalt destroy their name from under heaven: there shall no man be able to stand before thee, until thou have destroyed them. [25] The graven images of their gods shall ye burn with fire: thou shalt not desire the silver or gold that is on them, nor take it unto thee, lest thou be _____ therein: for it is an abomination to the Lord thy God. [26] Neither shalt thou _____ an _____ into thine _____ , lest thou be a _____ thing like it: but thou shalt utterly _____ it, and thou shalt utterly _____ it; for it is a _____ thing.

[8:1] _____ the _____ which I command thee this day shall ye _____ to _____ , that ye may _____ , and _____ , and go _____ and possess the land which the Lord sware unto your fathers. [2] And thou shalt _____ all the way which the Lord thy God led thee these _____ years in the wilderness, to humble thee, and to _____ thee, to _____ what was in thine _____ , whether thou wouldest keep his commandments, or no. [3] And he _____ thee, and suffered thee to _____ , and _____ thee with _____ , which thou knewest not, neither did thy fathers know; that he might make thee know that man doth _____ live by _____ only, but by every _____ that proceedeth out of the _____ of the _____ doth man live. [4] Thy _____ waxed not old upon thee, neither did thy _____ swell, these forty years. [5] Thou shalt also consider in thine _____ , that, as a man _____ his son, so the Lord thy God chasteneth thee. [6] Therefore thou shalt keep the _____ of the Lord thy God, to walk in his ways, and to _____ him. [7] For the Lord thy God bringeth thee into a good land, a land of brooks of water, of fountains and depths that spring out of valleys and hills; [8] A land of wheat, and barley, and vines, and fig trees, and pomegranates; a land of oil olive, and honey; [9] A land wherein thou shalt eat bread without scarceness, thou shalt not _____ any thing in it; a land whose stones are iron, and out of whose hills thou mayest dig brass. [10] When thou hast eaten and art full, then thou shalt _____ the Lord thy God for the good land which he hath given thee. [11] Beware that thou _____ not the Lord thy God, in not keeping his commandments, and his judgments, and his statutes, which I command thee this day: [12] Lest when thou hast eaten and art full, and hast built goodly houses, and dwelt therein; [13] And when thy herds and thy flocks multiply, and thy silver and thy gold is multiplied, and all that thou hast is multiplied; [14] Then thine _____ be lifted up, and thou _____ the Lord thy God, which brought thee forth out of the land of Egypt, from the house of _____ ; [15] Who led thee through that great and terrible wilderness, wherein were fiery serpents, and scorpions, and drought, where there was no water; who brought thee forth _____ out of the _____ of flint; [16] Who fed thee in the wilderness with _____ , which thy fathers knew not, that he might humble thee, and that he might prove thee, to do thee good at thy latter end; [17] And thou say in thine heart, My power and the might of mine hand hath gotten me this wealth. [18] But thou shalt _____ the Lord thy God: for it is _____ that giveth thee _____ to get _____ , that he may establish his covenant which he sware unto thy fathers, as it is this day. [19] And it shall be, if thou do at all _____ the Lord thy God, and walk after other _____ , and _____ them, and _____

DEUTERONOMY

them, I testify against you this day that ye shall surely _____ . [20] As the nations which the Lord destroyeth before your face, so shall ye perish; because ye would not be _____ unto the voice of the Lord your God.

[9:1] Hear, O Israel: Thou art to pass over Jordan this day, to go in to possess nations greater and mightier than thyself, cities great and fenced up to heaven, [2] A people great and tall, the children of the Anakims, whom thou knowest, and of whom thou hast heard say, Who can stand before the children of Anak! [3] _____ therefore this day, that the _____ thy God is he which goeth over before thee; as a _____ fire he shall destroy them, and he shall bring them down before thy face: so shalt thou _____ them out, and destroy them quickly, as the Lord hath said unto thee. [4] Speak not thou in thine heart, after that the Lord thy God hath cast them out from before thee, saying, For my _____ the Lord hath brought me in to possess this land: but for the _____ of these nations the Lord doth drive them _____ from before thee. [5] _____ for thy _____ , or for the _____ of thine heart, dost thou go to possess their land: but for the _____ of these nations the Lord thy God doth _____ them _____ from before thee, and that he may perform the word which the Lord sware unto thy fathers, _____ , _____ , and _____ . [6] Understand therefore, that the Lord thy God giveth thee not this _____ land to _____ it for thy righteousness; for thou art a _____ people.

[7] _____ , and forget not, how thou provokedst the Lord thy God to wrath in the wilderness: from the day that thou didst depart out of the land of Egypt, until ye came unto this place, ye have been _____ against the Lord. [8] Also in Horeb ye provoked the Lord to wrath, so that the Lord was _____ with you to have destroyed you. [9] When I was gone up into the mount to receive the tables of _____ , even the tables of the covenant which the Lord made with you, then I abode in the mount _____ days and _____ nights, I neither did eat bread nor drink water: [10] And the Lord delivered unto me two tables of stone written with the _____ of God; and on them was written according to all the words, which the Lord spake with you in the mount out of the midst of the fire in the day of the assembly. [11] And it came to pass at the end of forty days and forty nights, that the Lord gave me the two tables of stone, even the tables of the covenant. [12] And the Lord said unto me, Arise, get thee down quickly from hence; for thy people which thou hast brought forth out of Egypt have _____ themselves; they are quickly turned aside out of the way which I commanded them; they have made them a molten _____ . [13] Furthermore the Lord spake unto me, saying, I have seen this people, and, behold, it is a stiffnecked people: [14] Let me alone, that I may destroy them, and blot out their name from under heaven: and I will make of thee a nation mightier and greater than they. [15] So I turned and came down from the mount, and the mount burned with fire: and the two tables of the covenant were in my two hands. [16] And I looked, and, behold, ye had _____ against the Lord your God, and had made you a molten _____ : ye had turned aside quickly out of the way which the Lord had commanded you. [17] And I took the two tables, and _____ them out of my two hands, and _____ them before your eyes. [18] And I fell down before the Lord, as at the first, forty days and forty nights: I did neither eat bread, nor drink water, because of all your sins which ye sinned, in doing wickedly in the sight of the Lord, to provoke him to anger. [19] For I was _____ of the anger and hot displeasure, wherewith the Lord was wroth against you to destroy you. But the

DEUTERONOMY

Lord hearkened unto me at that time also. [20] And the Lord was very angry with _____ to have destroyed him: and I prayed for Aaron also the same time. [21] And I took your _____ , the calf which ye had made, and burnt it with fire, and stamped it, and ground it very small, even until it was as small as dust: and I cast the dust thereof into the brook that descended out of the mount. [22] And at Taberah, and at Massah, and at Kibroth-hattaavah, ye provoked the Lord to wrath. [23] Likewise when the Lord sent you from Kadesh-barnea, saying, Go up and possess the land which I have given you; then ye rebelled against the commandment of the Lord your God, and ye believed him not, nor hearkened to his voice. [24] Ye have been rebellious against the Lord from the day that I knew you. [25] Thus I fell down before the Lord forty days and forty nights, as I fell down at the first; because the Lord had said he would destroy you. [26] I _____ therefore unto the Lord, and said, O Lord God, destroy not thy people and thine inheritance, which thou hast _____ through thy greatness, which thou hast brought forth out of Egypt with a mighty hand. [27] Remember thy servants, Abraham, Isaac, and Jacob; look not unto the stubbornness of this people, nor to their wickedness, nor to their sin: [28] Lest the land whence thou broughtest us out say, Because the Lord was not able to bring them into the land which he promised them, and because he hated them, he hath brought them out to slay them in the wilderness. [29] Yet they are thy people and thine inheritance, which thou broughtest out by thy mighty power and by thy stretched out arm.

[10:1] At that time the Lord said unto me, _____ thee two _____ of stone _____ unto the first, and come up unto me into the mount, and _____ thee an _____ of _____ . [2] And I will write on the tables the words that were in the first tables which thou brakest, and thou shalt put them in the ark. [3] And I made an ark of shittim wood, and hewed two tables of stone like unto the first, and went up into the mount, having the two tables in mine hand. [4] And he _____ on the tables, according to the first writing, the _____ commandments, which the Lord spake unto you in the mount out of the midst of the fire in the day of the assembly: and the Lord gave them unto me. [5] And I turned myself and came down from the mount, and put the tables in the ark which I had made; and there they be, as the Lord commanded me.

[6] And the children of Israel took their journey from Beeroth of the children of Jaakan to Mosera: there Aaron _____ , and there he was _____ ; and _____ his son ministered in the priest's office in his stead. [7] From thence they journeyed unto Gudgodah; and from Gudgodah to Jotbath, a land of rivers of waters.

[8] At that time the Lord separated the tribe of _____ , to bear the ark of the covenant of the Lord, to stand before the Lord to _____ unto him, and to _____ in his name, unto this day. [9] Wherefore Levi hath no part nor inheritance with his brethren; the Lord is his inheritance, according as the Lord thy God promised him. [10] And I stayed in the mount, according to the first time, forty days and forty nights; and the Lord hearkened unto me at that time also, and the Lord would not destroy thee. [11] And the Lord said unto me, Arise, take thy journey before the people, that they may go in and possess the land, which I sware unto their fathers to give unto them.

[12] And now, Israel, _____ doth the Lord thy God _____ of thee, but to _____ the Lord thy God, to _____ in all his _____ , and to _____ him, and to _____ the Lord thy God with _____ thy _____ and with _____ thy _____ , [13] To _____ the

DEUTERONOMY

_____ of the Lord, and his _____ , which I command thee this day for thy good? [14] Behold, the _____ and the heaven of heavens is the _____ thy God, the _____ also, with _____ that _____ is. [15] Only the _____ had a _____ in thy fathers to _____ them, and he _____ their seed after them, even _____ above all people, as it is this day. [16] _____ therefore the foreskin of your _____ , and be no more stiffnecked. [17] For the Lord your God is _____ of _____ , and _____ of _____ , a great God, a mighty, and a terrible, which regardeth not persons, nor taketh reward: [18] He doth execute the judgment of the _____ and _____ , and _____ the _____ , in giving him food and raiment. [19] Love ye therefore the stranger: for ye were strangers in the land of Egypt. [20] Thou shalt _____ the Lord thy God; him shalt thou _____ , and to him shalt thou _____ , and swear by his name. [21] He is thy _____ , and he is thy _____ , that hath done for thee these great and terrible things, which thine eyes have seen. [22] Thy fathers went down into Egypt with _____ and _____ persons; and now the Lord thy God hath made thee as the _____ of _____ for multitude.

[11:1] Therefore thou shalt _____ the Lord thy God, and keep his charge, and his statutes, and his judgments, and his commandments, _____ . [2] And know ye this day: for I speak not with your children which have not known, and which have not seen the chastisement of the Lord your God, his greatness, his mighty hand, and his stretched out arm, [3] And his miracles, and his acts, which he did in the midst of Egypt unto Pharaoh the king of Egypt, and unto all his land; [4] And what he did unto the army of Egypt, unto their horses, and to their chariots; how he made the water of the Red sea to overflow them as they pursued after you, and how the Lord hath destroyed them unto this day; [5] And what he did unto you in the wilderness, until ye came into this place; [6] And what he did unto _____ and _____ , the sons of _____ , the son of Reuben: how the _____ opened her mouth, and _____ them up, and their _____ , and their tents, and all the substance that was in their possession, in the midst of all Israel: [7] But your eyes have seen all the great acts of the Lord which he did. [8] Therefore shall ye keep all the commandments which I command you this day, that ye may be _____ , and go in and possess the land, whither ye go to possess it; [9] And that ye may prolong your days in the land, which the Lord sware unto your fathers to give unto them and to their seed, a land that floweth with _____ and _____ .

[10] For the land, whither thou goest in to possess it, is not as the land of _____ , from whence ye came out, where thou _____ thy seed, and _____ it with thy _____ , as a garden of herbs: [11] But the land, whither ye go to possess it, is a land of _____ and _____ , and drinketh water of the _____ of heaven: [12] A land which the Lord thy God _____ for: the _____ of the Lord thy God are always upon it, from the beginning of the year even unto the end of the year.

[13] And it shall come to pass, if ye shall hearken _____ unto my commandments which I command you this day, to _____ the Lord your God, and to _____ him with _____ your _____ and with _____ your _____ , [14] That I will give you the _____ of your land in his _____ season, the _____ rain and the _____ rain, that thou mayest _____ in thy corn, and thy wine, and thine oil. [15] And I will _____ grass in thy fields for

DEUTERONOMY

thy cattle, that thou mayest eat and be _____ . [16] Take heed to yourselves, that your heart be not _____ , and ye turn aside, and serve other gods, and worship them; [17] And then the Lord's wrath be kindled against you, and he shut up the _____ , that there be no _____ , and that the land yield not her _____ ; and lest ye perish quickly from off the good land which the Lord giveth you.

[18] Therefore shall ye lay up these my words in your heart and in your soul, and bind them for a _____ upon your hand, that they may be as frontlets between your eyes. [19] And ye shall _____ them your _____ , speaking of them when thou _____ in thine _____ , and when thou _____ by the way, when thou _____ down, and when thou _____ up. [20] And thou shalt _____ them upon the _____ posts of thine _____ , and upon thy _____ : [21] That your days may be _____ , and the _____ of your _____ , in the land which the Lord sware unto your fathers to give them, as the days of heaven upon the earth.

[22] For if ye shall _____ _____ all these commandments which I command you, to _____ them, to _____ the Lord your God, to _____ in all his _____ , and to _____ unto him; [23] Then will the Lord drive out all these nations from before you, and ye shall possess greater nations and mightier than yourselves. [24] Every place whereon the soles of your _____ shall _____ shall be yours: from the wilderness and Lebanon, from the river, the river Euphrates, even unto the uttermost sea shall your coast be. [25] There shall no man be able to stand before you: for the Lord your God shall lay the _____ of you and the _____ of you upon all the land that ye shall tread upon, as he hath said unto you.

[26] Behold, I set before you this day a _____ and a _____ ; [27] A blessing, _____ ye _____ the commandments of the Lord your God, which I command you this day: [28] And a _____ , if ye will _____ _____ the commandments of the Lord your God, but turn aside out of the way which I command you this day, to go after other _____ , which ye have not known. [29] And it shall come to pass, when the Lord thy God hath brought thee in unto the land whither thou goest to possess it, that thou shalt put the _____ upon mount _____ , and the _____ upon mount _____ . [30] Are they not on the _____ side Jordan, by the way where the sun goeth down, in the land of the Canaanites, which dwell in the champaign over against Gilgal, beside the plains of Moreh? [31] For ye shall pass over Jordan to go in to possess the land which the Lord your God giveth you, and ye shall possess it, and dwell therein. [32] And ye shall observe to do all the statutes and judgments which I set before you this day.

[12:1] These are the statutes and judgments, which ye shall observe to do in the land, which the Lord God of thy fathers giveth thee to possess it, all the days that ye live upon the earth. [2] Ye shall utterly _____ all the places, wherein the nations which ye shall possess served their gods, upon the high mountains, and upon the hills, and under every green tree: [3] And ye shall _____ their _____ , and break their pillars, and burn their groves with fire; and ye shall hew down the _____ images of their gods, and _____ the _____ of them out of that place. [4] Ye shall not do so unto the Lord your God. [5] But unto the place which the Lord your God shall choose out of all your tribes to put his name there, even unto his _____ shall ye _____ , and thither thou shalt come: [6] And thither ye shall _____ your burnt _____

DEUTERONOMY

, and your _____ , and your _____ , and _____ offerings of your hand, and your _____ , and your freewill _____ , and the _____ of your herds and of your flocks: [7] And there ye shall eat before the Lord your God, and ye shall _____ in all that ye put your hand unto, ye and your households, wherein the Lord thy God hath blessed thee. [8] Ye shall not do after all the things that we do here this day, every man whatsoever is right in his own eyes. [9] For ye are _____ as yet come to the _____ and to the _____ , which the Lord your God giveth you. [10] But when ye go over Jordan, and dwell in the land which the Lord your God giveth you to inherit, and when he giveth you rest from all your enemies round about, so that ye dwell in _____ ; [11] Then there shall be a place which the Lord your God shall choose to cause his name to dwell there; thither shall ye bring all that I command you; your burnt offerings, and your sacrifices, your tithes, and the heave offering of your hand, and all your choice vows which ye vow unto the Lord: [12] And ye shall _____ before the Lord your God, ye, and your sons, and your daughters, and your menservants, and your maidservants, and the Levite that is within your gates; forasmuch as he hath no part nor inheritance with you. [13] Take heed to thyself that thou offer not thy burnt offerings in every place that thou seest: [14] But in the place which the Lord shall choose in one of thy tribes, there thou shalt offer thy burnt offerings, and there thou shalt do all that I command thee. [15] Notwithstanding thou mayest _____ and _____ flesh in all thy _____ , whatsoever thy soul lusteth after, according to the blessing of the Lord thy God which he hath given thee: the unclean and the clean may eat thereof, as of the _____ , and as of the _____ . [16] Only ye shall _____ eat the _____ ; ye shall pour it upon the earth as water.

[17] Thou mayest not eat within thy gates the tithe of thy corn, or of thy wine, or of thy oil, or the firstlings of thy herds or of thy flock, nor any of thy vows which thou vowest, nor thy freewill offerings, or heave offering of thine hand: [18] But thou must eat them before the Lord thy God in the place which the Lord thy God shall choose, thou, and thy son, and thy daughter, and thy manservant, and thy maidservant, and the Levite that is within thy gates: and thou shalt rejoice before the Lord thy God in all that thou puttest thine hands unto. [19] Take heed to thyself that thou _____ _____ the _____ as long as thou livest upon the earth.

[20] When the Lord thy God shall enlarge thy border, as he hath promised thee, and thou shalt say, I will eat flesh, because thy soul longeth to eat flesh; thou mayest eat flesh, whatsoever thy soul lusteth after. [21] If the place which the Lord thy God hath chosen to put his name there be too far from thee, then thou shalt kill of thy herd and of thy flock, which the Lord hath given thee, as I have commanded thee, and thou shalt eat in thy gates whatsoever thy soul lusteth after. [22] Even as the roebuck and the hart is eaten, so thou shalt eat them: the unclean and the clean shall eat of them alike. [23] Only be sure that thou eat not the blood: for the _____ is the _____ ; and thou mayest not eat the life with the flesh. [24] Thou shalt not eat it; thou shalt _____ it upon the _____ as _____ . [25] Thou shalt not eat it; that it may go well with thee, and with thy children after thee, when thou shalt do that which is right in the sight of the Lord. [26] Only thy _____ things which thou hast, and thy vows, thou shalt take, and go unto the place which the Lord shall choose: [27] And thou shalt offer thy burnt offerings, the flesh and the blood, upon the altar of the Lord thy God: and the blood of thy sacrifices shall be poured out upon the altar of the Lord thy God, and thou shalt eat

DEUTERONOMY

the flesh. [28] _____ and _____ all these words which I command thee, that it may go well with thee, and with thy children after thee for ever, when thou doest that which is good and right in the sight of the Lord thy God.

[29] When the Lord thy God shall cut off the nations from before thee, whither thou goest to possess them, and thou succeedest them, and dwellest in their land; [30] Take heed to thyself that thou be not snared by following them, after that they be destroyed from before thee; and that thou enquire not after their gods, saying, How did these nations serve their gods? even so will I do likewise. [31] Thou shalt not do so unto the Lord thy God: for every _____ to the Lord, which he _____ , have they done unto their gods; for even their sons and their daughters they have burnt in the fire to their gods. [32] What thing soever I command you, observe to do it: thou shalt _____ _____ thereto, nor _____ from it.

[13:1] If there arise among you a _____ , or a _____ of dreams, and giveth thee a _____ or a _____ , [2] And the sign or the wonder come to _____ , whereof he spake unto thee, saying, Let us go after other gods, which thou hast not known, and let us serve them; [3] Thou shalt _____ hearken unto the words of that prophet, or that dreamer of dreams: for the Lord your God proveth you, to know whether ye _____ the Lord your God with all your _____ and with all your _____ . [4] Ye shall _____ after the Lord your God, and _____ him, and _____ his commandments, and _____ his voice, and ye shall _____ him, and _____ unto him. [5] And that prophet, or that dreamer of dreams, shall be put to _____ ; because he hath spoken to _____ you _____ from the Lord your God, which brought you out of the land of Egypt, and _____ you out of the house of bondage, to thrust thee out of the _____ which the Lord thy God commanded thee to _____ in. So shalt thou put the _____ away from the midst of thee.

[6] If thy _____ , the son of thy mother, or thy son, or thy daughter, or the wife of thy bosom, or thy friend, which is as thine own soul, _____ thee _____ , saying, Let us go and _____ other _____ , which thou hast not known, thou, nor thy fathers; [7] Namely, of the gods of the people which are round about you, nigh unto thee, or far off from thee, from the one end of the earth even unto the other end of the earth; [8] Thou shalt _____ _____ unto him, nor _____ unto him; neither shall thine eye _____ him, neither shalt thou _____ , neither shalt thou _____ him: [9] But thou shalt surely _____ him; thine hand shall be first upon him to put him to _____ , and afterwards the hand of _____ the _____ . [10] And thou shalt _____ him with stones, that he _____ ; because he hath sought to _____ thee away from the Lord thy God, which brought thee out of the land of Egypt, from the house of _____ . [11] And all Israel shall _____ , and _____ , and shall do _____ more any such _____ as this is among you.

[12] If thou shalt _____ say in one of thy cities, which the Lord thy God hath given thee to dwell there, saying, [13] Certain men, the children of Belial, are gone out from among you, and have withdrawn the inhabitants of their city, saying, Let us go and _____ other _____ , which ye have not known; [14] Then shalt thou _____ , and make _____ , and ask _____ ; and, behold, if it be _____ , and the thing certain, that such _____ is wrought among you; [15]

DEUTERONOMY

Thou shalt surely _____ the inhabitants of that _____ with the edge of the sword, _____ it utterly, and all that is therein, and the cattle thereof, with the edge of the sword. [16] And thou shalt gather all the spoil of it into the midst of the street thereof, and shalt _____ with fire the city, and all the spoil thereof every whit, for the Lord thy God: and it shall be an heap for ever; it shall not be built again. [17] And there shall cleave nought of the cursed thing to thine hand: that the Lord may turn from the fierceness of his anger, and shew thee mercy, and have compassion upon thee, and multiply thee, as he hath sworn unto thy fathers; [18] When thou shalt hearken to the voice of the Lord thy God, to keep all his commandments which I command thee this day, to do that which is _____ in the eyes of the Lord thy God.

[14:1] Ye are the _____ of the Lord your God: ye shall not _____ yourselves, nor make any _____ between your eyes _____ the _____ . [2] For thou art an holy people unto the Lord thy God, and the Lord hath chosen thee to be a peculiar people unto himself, _____ all the nations that are upon the earth.

[3] Thou shalt not _____ any _____ thing. [4] These are the _____ which ye shall eat: the _____ , the _____ , and the _____ , [5] The _____ , and the _____ , and the fallow _____ , and the _____ goat, and the _____ , and the _____ ox, and the _____ . [6] And every beast that _____ the _____ , and _____ the _____ into _____ claws, _____ cheweth the _____ among the beasts, that ye _____ eat. [7] Nevertheless these ye shall _____ eat of them that _____ the cud, or of them that _____ the cloven hoof; as the _____ , and the _____ , and the _____ : for they _____ the cud, but divide _____ the hoof; therefore they are _____ unto you. [8] And the _____ , because it _____ the hoof, yet cheweth _____ the _____ , it is _____ unto you: ye shall _____ eat of their _____ , nor touch their dead carcase.

[9] These ye _____ eat of _____ that are in the _____ : all that have _____ and _____ shall ye eat: [10] And whatsoever hath _____ fins and scales ye may _____ eat; it is _____ unto you.

[11] Of all _____ birds ye shall eat. [12] But these are they of which ye shall _____ eat: the _____ , and _____ , and the _____ , [13] And the _____ , and the _____ , and the _____ after his kind, [14] And every _____ after his kind, [15] And the _____ , and the _____ hawk, and the _____ , and the _____ after his kind, [16] The _____ owl, and the _____ owl, and the _____ , [17] And the _____ , and the _____ eagle, and the _____ , [18] And the _____ , and the _____ after her kind, and the _____ , and the _____ . [19] And every _____ thing that _____ is unclean unto you: they shall _____ be eaten. [20] But of all _____ fowls ye may eat.

[21] Ye shall _____ eat of any thing that _____ of itself: thou shalt _____ it unto the _____ that is in thy gates, that he may eat it; or thou _____ sell it unto an _____ : for thou art an _____ people unto the Lord thy God. Thou shalt not _____ a kid in his _____ milk. [22] Thou shalt truly _____ all the _____ of thy _____ , that the field bringeth forth year by year. [23] And thou shalt _____ before the Lord thy God, in the

DEUTERONOMY

_____ which he shall choose to place his name there, the _____ of thy _____ , of thy _____ , and of thine _____ , and the _____ of thy _____ and of thy _____ ; that thou mayest _____ to fear the Lord thy God always. [24] And if the way be too _____ for thee, so that thou art not _____ to carry it; or if the place be too _____ from thee, which the Lord thy God shall choose to set his name there, when the Lord thy God hath _____ thee: [25] Then shalt thou _____ it into _____ , and _____ up the money in thine hand, and shalt go unto the place which the Lord thy God shall choose: [26] And thou shalt _____ that money for whatsoever thy soul lusteth after, for _____ , or for _____ , or for _____ , or for strong _____ , or for whatsoever thy soul desireth: and thou shalt _____ there before the Lord thy God, and thou shalt _____ , thou, and thine household, [27] And the Levite that is within thy gates; thou shalt _____ forsake him; for he hath no part nor inheritance with thee.

[28] At the end of _____ years thou shalt bring forth all the _____ of thine _____ the same year, and shalt lay it up within thy gates: [29] And the _____ , (because he hath no part nor inheritance with thee,) and the stranger, and the fatherless, and the widow, which are within thy gates, shall come, and shall eat and be _____ ; that the Lord thy God may bless thee in all the work of thine hand which thou doest.

[15:1] At the end of every _____ years thou shalt make a _____ . [2] And this is the _____ of the release: Every _____ that lendeth ought unto his neighbour shall _____ it; he shall not _____ it of his neighbour, or of his brother; because it is called the _____ release. [3] Of a _____ thou mayest _____ it again: but that which is thine with thy brother thine hand shall release; [4] Save when there shall be no poor among you; for the Lord shall greatly bless thee in the land which the Lord thy God giveth thee for an inheritance to possess it: [5] Only if thou carefully _____ unto the voice of the Lord thy God, to _____ to do all these commandments which I command thee this day. [6] For the Lord thy God blesseth thee, as he promised thee: and thou shalt _____ unto many nations, but thou shalt _____ borrow; and thou shalt _____ over many _____ ,but they shall not _____ over thee.

[7] If there be among you a _____ man of one of thy brethren within any of thy gates in thy land which the Lord thy God giveth thee, thou shalt not _____ thine heart, nor shut thine _____ from thy poor brother: [8] But thou shalt _____ thine hand wide unto him, and shalt surely _____ him sufficient for his need, in that which he wanteth. [9] Beware that there be not a _____ in thy _____ heart, saying, The _____ year, the year of release, is at hand; and thine eye be evil against thy poor brother, and thou givest him _____ ; and he _____ unto the Lord against thee, and it be _____ unto thee. [10] Thou shalt surely _____ him, and thine _____ shall not be grieved when thou givest unto him: because that for this thing the Lord thy God shall _____ thee in all thy _____ , and in all that thou puttest thine hand unto. [11] For the poor shall never _____ out of the land: therefore I command thee, saying, Thou shalt _____ thine _____ wide unto thy brother, to thy _____ , and to thy _____ , in thy land.

[12] And if thy brother, an _____ man, or an _____ woman, be _____ unto thee, and serve thee _____ years; then in the _____ year thou shalt let him go _____ from thee. [13] And when thou sendest him out free

DEUTERONOMY

from thee, thou shalt not let him go away _____ : [14] Thou shalt _____ him _____ out of thy _____ , and out of thy _____ , and out of thy _____ : of that wherewith the _____ thy God hath _____ thee thou shalt _____ unto him. [15] And thou shalt _____ that thou wast a bondman in the land of Egypt, and the Lord thy God _____ thee: therefore I command thee this thing to day. [16] And it shall be, if he say unto thee, I will not go away from thee; because he _____ thee and thine house, because he is well with thee; [17] Then thou shalt take an _____ , and _____ it through his _____ unto the door, and he shall be thy servant for ever. And also unto thy maidservant thou shalt do likewise. [18] It shall not seem hard unto thee, when thou sendest him away free from thee; for he hath been worth a _____ hired servant to thee, in serving thee _____ years: and the Lord thy God shall bless thee in all that thou doest.

[19] All the firstling males that come of thy herd and of thy flock thou shalt sanctify unto the Lord thy God: thou shalt do no _____ with the firstling of thy bullock, nor shear the firstling of thy sheep. [20] Thou shalt _____ it before the Lord thy God year by year in the place which the Lord shall choose, thou and thy household. [21] And if there be any _____ therein, as if it be _____ , or _____ , or have any _____ blemish, thou shalt _____ sacrifice it unto the Lord thy God. [22] Thou shalt _____ it within thy gates: the _____ and the _____ person shall eat it alike, as the _____ , and as the _____ . [23] Only thou shalt _____ eat the _____ thereof; thou shalt _____ it upon the ground as water.

[16:1] Observe the month of _____ , and keep the _____ unto the Lord thy God: for in the month of _____ the Lord thy God brought thee forth out of _____ by night. [2] Thou shalt therefore sacrifice the _____ unto the Lord thy God, of the flock and the herd, in the place which the Lord shall choose to place his name there. [3] Thou shalt eat no _____ bread with it; _____ days shalt thou eat _____ bread therewith, even the bread of _____ ; for thou camest forth out of the land of Egypt in _____ : that thou mayest _____ the day when thou camest forth out of the land of Egypt all the days of thy life. [4] And there shall be no _____ bread seen with thee in all thy coast _____ days; neither shall there any thing of the _____ , which thou sacrificedst the first day at even, remain all _____ until the morning. [5] Thou mayest not sacrifice the _____ within any of thy _____ , which the Lord thy God giveth thee: [6] But at the place which the Lord thy God shall choose to place his name in, there thou shalt sacrifice the _____ at even, at the going down of the _____ , at the season that thou camest forth out of Egypt. [7] And thou shalt _____ and eat it in the place which the Lord thy God shall choose: and thou shalt turn in the morning, and go unto thy _____ . [8] _____ days thou shalt eat unleavened bread: and on the _____ day shall be a _____ assembly to the Lord thy God: thou shalt do _____ work therein.

[9] _____ weeks shalt thou number unto thee: begin to number the seven weeks from such time as thou beginnest to put the _____ to the corn. [10] And thou shalt keep the feast of weeks unto the Lord thy God with a _____ of a freewill offering of thine hand, which thou shalt _____ unto the Lord thy God, according as the Lord thy God hath blessed thee: [11] And thou shalt _____ before the Lord thy God, thou, and thy son, and thy daughter, and thy manservant, and thy maidservant, and

DEUTERONOMY

the Levite that is within thy gates, and the stranger, and the fatherless, and the widow, that are among you, in the place which the Lord thy God hath chosen to place his name there. [12] And thou shalt _____ that thou wast a bondman in Egypt: and thou shalt _____ and _____ these _____ .

[13] Thou shalt _____ the feast of _____ seven days, after that thou hast gathered in thy corn and thy wine: [14] And thou shalt _____ in thy feast, thou, and thy son, and thy daughter, and thy manservant, and thy maidservant, and the Levite, the stranger, and the fatherless, and the widow, that are within thy gates. [15] _____ days shalt thou keep a solemn _____ unto the Lord thy God in the place which the Lord shall choose: because the Lord thy God shall _____ thee in all thine increase, and in all the works of thine hands, therefore thou shalt surely _____ .

[16] _____ times in a year shall all thy males appear before the Lord thy God in the place which he shall choose; in the _____ of _____ bread, and in the _____ of _____ , and in the _____ of _____ : and they shall _____ appear before the Lord _____ : [17] Every man shall _____ as he is _____ , according to the _____ of the Lord thy God which he hath given thee.

[18] _____ and _____ shalt thou make thee in all thy gates, which the Lord thy God giveth thee, throughout thy tribes: and they shall _____ the people with _____ judgment. [19] Thou shalt not _____ judgment; thou shalt not _____ persons, neither take a _____ : for a gift doth _____ the _____ of the _____ , and _____ the _____ of the _____ . [20] That which is _____ just shalt thou _____ , that thou mayest _____ , and inherit the land which the Lord thy God _____ thee.

[21] Thou shalt _____ plant thee a _____ of any trees near unto the _____ of the Lord thy God, which thou shalt make thee. [22] Neither shalt thou _____ thee up any _____ ; which the Lord thy God _____ .

[17:1] Thou shalt not _____ unto the Lord thy God any bullock, or sheep, wherein is _____ , or any _____ : for that is an _____ unto the Lord thy God.

[2] If there be found among you, within any of thy gates which the Lord thy God giveth thee, man or woman, that hath wrought _____ in the sight of the Lord thy God, in transgressing his covenant, [3] And hath gone and served other _____ , and _____ them, either the sun, or moon, or any of the host of heaven, which I have not commanded; [4] And it be told thee, and thou hast heard of it, and enquired diligently, and, behold, it be _____ , and the thing certain, that such abomination is wrought in Israel: [5] Then shalt thou _____ forth that man or that woman, which have committed that wicked thing, unto thy gates, even that man or that woman, and shalt stone them with stones, till they _____ . [6] At the mouth of _____ witnesses, or _____ witnesses, shall he that is worthy of death be put to death; but at the mouth of _____ witness he shall _____ be put to death. [7] The hands of the _____ shall be _____ upon him to put him to death, and afterward the hands of all the people. So thou shalt put the _____ away from among you.

[8] If there arise a matter too _____ for thee in judgment, between _____ and blood, between plea and _____ , and between _____ and stroke, being matters of _____ within thy gates: then shalt thou _____ , and get thee up

DEUTERONOMY

into the place which the Lord thy God shall choose; [9] And thou shalt come unto the _____ the Levites, and unto the judge that shall be in those days, and enquire; and they shall shew thee the _____ of judgment: [10] And thou shalt do according to the sentence, which they of that place which the Lord shall _____ shall shew thee; and thou shalt _____ to do according to _____ that they inform thee: [11] According to the sentence of the law which they shall _____ thee, and according to the _____ which they shall tell thee, thou shalt do: thou shalt not _____ from the sentence which they shall shew thee, to the right hand, nor to the left. [12] And the man that will do _____ , and will _____ hearken unto the _____ that standeth to minister there _____ the _____ thy God, or unto the judge, even that man shall die: and thou shalt put away the evil from Israel. [13] And all the people shall _____ , and _____ , and do _____ more presumptuously.

[14] When thou art come unto the land which the Lord thy God giveth thee, and shalt possess it, and shalt dwell therein, and shalt say, I will set a _____ over me, like as all the nations that are about me; [15] Thou shalt in any wise set him king over thee, whom the Lord thy God shall _____ : one from among thy _____ shalt thou set king over thee: thou mayest not set a stranger over thee, which is not thy brother. [16] But he shall not multiply _____ to himself, nor _____ the people to return to _____ , to the end that he should multiply horses: forasmuch as the Lord hath said unto you, Ye shall henceforth return no more that _____ . [17] Neither shall he multiply _____ to himself, that his heart turn not away: neither shall he greatly multiply to himself _____ and gold. [18] And it shall be, when he sitteth upon the throne of his kingdom, that he shall _____ him a copy of this _____ in a book out of that which is before the priests the Levites: [19] And it shall be with him, and he shall _____ therein all the _____ of his life: that he may _____ to fear the Lord his God, to keep all the words of this law and these statutes, to do them: [20] That his heart be not _____ up above his brethren, and that he turn not aside from the commandment, to the right hand, or to the left: to the end that he may prolong his days in his kingdom, he, and his children, in the midst of Israel.

[18:1] The priests the Levites, and all the tribe of Levi, shall have no part nor inheritance with Israel: they shall _____ the offerings of the Lord made by fire, and his inheritance. [2] Therefore shall they have no _____ among their brethren: the _____ is their inheritance, as he hath said unto them.

[3] And this shall be the priest's _____ from the people, from them that offer a sacrifice, whether it be ox or sheep; and they shall give unto the priest the _____ , and the two _____ , and the _____ . [4] The _____ also of thy _____ , of thy _____ , and of thine _____ , and the first of the _____ of thy sheep, shalt thou give him. [5] For the Lord thy God hath _____ him out of all thy tribes, to _____ to _____ in the name of the Lord, _____ and his _____ for ever.

[6] And if a Levite come from any of thy gates out of all Israel, where he sojourned, and come with all the desire of his mind unto the place which the Lord shall choose; [7] Then he shall minister in the name of the Lord his God, as all his brethren the Levites do, which stand there before the Lord. [8] They shall have like portions to eat, beside that which cometh of the sale of his patrimony.

DEUTERONOMY

[9] When thou art come into the land which the Lord thy God giveth thee, thou shalt not _____ to do after the _____ of those nations. [10] There shall _____ be found among you any one that _____ his son or his daughter to pass through the _____ , or that useth _____ , or an _____ of times, or an _____ , or a _____ , [11] Or a _____ , or a _____ with familiar _____ , or a _____ , or a _____ . [12] For all that do these things are an _____ unto the Lord: and because of these abominations the Lord thy God doth drive them out from before thee. [13] Thou shalt be _____ with the Lord thy God. [14] For these nations, which thou shalt possess, hearkened unto observers of times, and unto diviners: but as for thee, the Lord thy God hath not suffered thee so to do.

[15] The Lord thy God will raise up unto thee a _____ from the midst of thee, of thy brethren, like unto me; unto him ye shall hearken; [16] According to all that thou desiredst of the Lord thy God in Horeb in the day of the assembly, saying, Let me not hear again the voice of the Lord my God, neither let me see this great fire any more, that I die not. [17] And the Lord said unto me, They have well spoken that which they have spoken. [18] I will raise them up a _____ from among their brethren, like unto thee, and will put my words in his mouth; and he shall speak unto them all that I shall command him. [19] And it shall come to pass, that whosoever will _____ hearken unto my _____ which he shall speak in my _____ , I will require it of him. [20] But the _____ , which shall presume to speak a word in my name, which I have _____ commanded him to speak, or that shall speak in the name of other _____ , even that prophet shall _____ . [21] And if thou say in thine _____ , How shall we _____ the word which the Lord hath not spoken? [22] When a prophet speaketh in the _____ of the Lord, if the thing follow _____ , nor come to pass, that is the thing which the Lord hath _____ spoken, but the prophet hath spoken it _____ : thou shalt _____ be afraid of him.

[19:1] When the Lord thy God hath cut off the nations, whose land the Lord thy God giveth thee, and thou succeedest them, and dwellest in their cities, and in their houses; [2] Thou shalt separate _____ cities for thee in the midst of thy land, which the Lord thy God giveth thee to possess it. [3] Thou shalt _____ thee a _____ , and divide the coasts of thy land, which the Lord thy God giveth thee to inherit, into three parts, that every slayer may flee thither.

[4] And this is the case of the _____ , which shall flee thither, that he may live: Whoso killeth his neighbour _____ , whom he hated not in time past; [5] As when a man goeth into the wood with his neighbour to hew wood, and his hand fetcheth a stroke with the axe to cut down the tree, and the head _____ from the helve, and lighteth upon his neighbour, that he die; he shall flee unto one of those cities, and live: [6] Lest the avenger of the blood pursue the slayer, while his heart is _____ , and overtake him, because the way is long, and slay him; whereas he was not worthy of death, inasmuch as he hated him not in time past. [7] Wherefore I command thee, saying, Thou shalt separate three cities for thee. [8] And if the Lord thy God _____ thy coast, as he hath sworn unto thy fathers, and give thee all the land which he promised to give unto thy fathers; [9] If thou shalt keep all these commandments to do them, which I command thee this day, to _____ the Lord thy God, and to _____ ever in his ways; then shalt thou add three cities more for thee, beside these three: [10] That

DEUTERONOMY

_____ blood be not shed in thy land, which the Lord thy God giveth thee for an inheritance, and so blood be upon thee.

[11] But if any man _____ his neighbour, and lie in wait for him, and rise up against him, and smite him mortally that he die, and fleeth into one of these cities: [12] Then the elders of his city shall send and fetch him thence, and deliver him into the hand of the avenger of blood, that he may die. [13] Thine eye shall not _____ him, but thou shalt put away the guilt of innocent blood from Israel, that it may go well with thee.

[14] Thou shalt not remove thy neighbour's _____ , which they of old time have set in thine inheritance, which thou shalt inherit in the land that the Lord thy God giveth thee to possess it.

[15] One witness shall not rise up against a man for any iniquity, or for any sin, in any sin that he sinneth: at the mouth of _____ witnesses, or at the mouth of _____ witnesses, shall the matter be _____ .

[16] If a _____ witness rise up against any man to testify against him that which is wrong; [17] Then both the men, between whom the controversy is, shall stand before the Lord, before the priests and the judges, which shall be in those days; [18] And the judges shall make diligent inquisition: and, behold, if the witness be a _____ witness, and hath testified falsely against his brother; [19] Then shall ye _____ unto him, as he had _____ to have done unto his brother: so shalt thou put the evil away from among you. [20] And those which remain shall _____ , and _____ , and shall henceforth _____ no more any such evil among you. [21] And thine eye shall not _____ ; but _____ shall go for _____ , _____ for _____ , _____ for _____ , _____ for _____ , _____ for _____ .

[20:1] When thou goest out to battle against thine enemies, and seest horses, and chariots, and a people more than thou, be not _____ of them: for the _____ thy God is _____ thee, which brought thee up out of the land of Egypt. [2] And it shall be, when ye are come nigh unto the battle, that the _____ shall approach and speak unto the people, [3] And shall say unto them, Hear, O Israel, ye approach this day unto battle against your enemies: let not your hearts _____ , fear not, and do not tremble, neither be ye terrified because of them; [4] For the Lord your God is he that goeth with you, to _____ for you against your enemies, to save you.

[5] And the officers shall speak unto the people, saying, What man is there that hath built a new house, and hath not _____ it? let him go and return to his house, lest he die in the battle, and another man dedicate it. [6] And what man is he that hath planted a vineyard, and hath not yet _____ of it? let him also go and return unto his house, lest he die in the battle, and another man eat of it. [7] And what man is there that hath betrothed a _____ , and hath not taken her? let him go and return unto his house, lest he die in the battle, and another man take her. [8] And the officers shall speak further unto the people, and they shall say, What man is there that is _____ and _____ ? let him _____ and return unto his house, lest his brethren's heart faint as well as his heart. [9] And it shall be, when the officers have made an end of speaking unto the people, that they shall make _____ of the armies to lead the people.

[10] When thou comest nigh unto a city to fight against it, then proclaim _____ unto it. [11] And it shall be, if it make thee answer of peace, and open unto thee, then it

DEUTERONOMY

shall be, that all the people that is found therein shall be _____ unto thee, and they shall _____ thee. [12] And if it will make no peace with thee, but will make _____ against thee, then thou shalt _____ it: [13] And when the Lord thy God hath delivered it into thine hands, thou shalt smite every _____ thereof with the edge of the sword: [14] But the women, and the little ones, and the cattle, and all that is in the city, even all the spoil thereof, shalt thou take unto thyself; and thou shalt eat the spoil of thine enemies, which the Lord thy God hath given thee. [15] Thus shalt thou do unto all the cities which are very far off from thee, which are not of the cities of these nations. [16] But of the cities of these people, which the Lord thy God doth give thee for an inheritance, thou shalt save _____ nothing that _____ : [17] But thou shalt utterly destroy them; namely, the Hittites, and the Amorites, the Canaanites, and the Perizzites, the Hivites, and the Jebusites; as the Lord thy God hath commanded thee: [18] That they teach you not to do after all their abominations, which they have done unto their _____ ; so should ye sin against the Lord your God.

[19] When thou shalt besiege a city a long time, in making war against it to take it, thou shalt not _____ the trees thereof by forcing an axe against them: for thou mayest eat of them, and thou shalt _____ cut them down (for the _____ of the field is man's _____) to employ them in the siege: [20] Only the trees which thou knowest that they be not trees for meat, thou shalt _____ and cut them down; and thou shalt build bulwarks against the city that maketh war with thee, until it be subdued.

[21:1] If one be found _____ in the land which the Lord thy God giveth thee to possess it, lying in the field, and it be not known who hath slain him: [2] Then thy elders and thy judges shall come forth, and they shall measure unto the cities which are round about him that is slain: [3] And it shall be, that the city which is next unto the slain man, even the elders of that city shall take an heifer, which hath not been wrought with, and which hath not drawn in the yoke; [4] And the elders of that city shall bring down the heifer unto a rough valley, which is neither eared nor sown, and shall strike off the heifer's _____ there in the valley: [5] And the _____ the sons of Levi shall come near; for them the Lord thy God hath _____ to _____ unto him, and to _____ in the name of the Lord; and by their _____ shall every controversy and every stroke be tried: [6] And all the elders of that city, that are next unto the slain man, shall _____ their hands over the heifer that is beheaded in the valley: [7] And they shall _____ and say, Our hands have not shed this blood, neither have our _____ seen it. [8] Be _____ , O Lord, unto thy people Israel, whom thou hast _____ , and lay not innocent blood unto thy people of Israel's charge. And the blood shall be _____ them. [9] So shalt thou put away the _____ of innocent blood from among you, when thou shalt do that which is _____ in the sight of the Lord.

[10] When thou goest forth to _____ against thine enemies, and the Lord thy God hath delivered them into thine hands, and thou hast taken them _____ , [11] And seest among the captives a _____ woman, and hast a _____ unto her, that thou wouldest have her to thy _____ ; [12] Then thou shalt bring her home to thine _____ ; and she shall _____ her head, and pare her _____ ; [13] And she shall put the _____ of her captivity from _____ her, and shall remain in thine _____ , and bewail her father and her mother a full _____ :

DEUTERONOMY

and after that thou shalt go _____ unto her, and be her _____, and she shall be thy _____. [14] And it shall be, if thou have no _____ in her, then thou shalt let her go whither she will; but thou shalt not sell her at all for _____, thou shalt not make merchandise of her, because thou hast _____ her.

   [15] If a man have _____ wives, one beloved, and another hated, and they have born him children, both the _____ and the _____; and if the firstborn son be hers that was hated: [16] Then it shall be, when he maketh his sons to _____ that which he hath, that he may not make the son of the beloved firstborn before the son of the hated, which is indeed the firstborn: [17] But he shall _____ the son of the hated for the _____, by giving him a _____ portion of all that he hath: for he is the beginning of his _____; the _____ of the firstborn is _____.

   [18] If a man have a _____ and _____ son, which will not _____ the voice of his father, or the voice of his mother, and that, when they have _____ him, will not _____ unto them: [19] Then shall his father and his mother _____ hold on him, and bring him out unto the _____ of his city, and unto the _____ of his place; [20] And they shall say unto the elders of his city, This our _____ is stubborn and rebellious, he will _____ obey our voice; he is a _____, and a _____. [21] And all the men of his city shall _____ him with stones, that he _____: so shalt thou put evil away from among you; and all Israel shall hear, and fear.

   [22] And if a man have committed a sin worthy of _____, and he be to be put to _____, and thou hang him on a tree: [23] His body shall _____ remain all _____ upon the tree, but thou shalt in any wise _____ him that day; (for he that is hanged is _____ of God;) that thy land be not defiled, which the Lord thy God giveth thee for an inheritance.

   [22:1] Thou shalt not see the _____ ox or his sheep go _____, and hide thyself from them: thou shalt in any case _____ them again unto thy brother. [2] And if thy brother be not _____ unto thee, or if thou know him not, then thou shalt bring it unto thine own house, and it shall be with thee until thy brother _____ after it, and thou shalt _____ it to him again. [3] In like manner shalt thou do with his ass; and so shalt thou do with his raiment; and with all _____ things of thy brother's, which he hath lost, and thou hast _____, shalt thou do likewise: thou mayest not hide thyself.

   [4] Thou shalt _____ see thy brother's ass or his ox _____ down by the way, and _____ thyself from them: thou shalt surely _____ him to lift them up again.

   [5] The _____ shall not _____ that which _____ unto a man, neither shall a _____ put on a woman's _____: for all that _____ so are _____ unto the Lord thy God.

   [6] If a bird's nest chance to be before thee in the way in any tree, or on the ground, whether they be young ones, or eggs, and the dam sitting upon the young, or upon the eggs, thou shalt not take the dam with the young: [7] But thou shalt in any wise let the dam go, and take the young to thee; that it may be well with thee, and that thou mayest prolong thy days.

   [8] When thou buildest a new _____, then thou shalt make a battlement for thy roof, that thou bring not blood upon thine house, if any man _____ from thence.

DEUTERONOMY

[9] Thou shalt _____ sow thy vineyard with divers seeds: lest the fruit of thy seed which thou hast sown, and the fruit of thy vineyard, be _____ .

[10] Thou shalt not _____ with an ox and an ass together.

[11] Thou shalt not _____ a garment of divers sorts, as of woollen and linen together.

[12] Thou shalt make thee _____ upon the four quarters of thy vesture, wherewith thou coverest thyself.

[13] If any man take a _____ , and go in unto her, and _____ her, [14] And give occasions of _____ against her, and bring up an evil _____ upon her, and say, I took this woman, and when I came to her, I found her not a _____ : [15] Then shall the father of the damsel, and her mother, take and bring forth the _____ of the damsel's _____ unto the elders of the city in the gate: [16] And the damsel's father shall say unto the elders, I gave my daughter unto this man to wife, and he hateth her; [17] And, lo, he hath given occasions of speech against her, saying, I found not thy daughter a maid; and yet these are the tokens of my daughter's _____ . And they shall spread the cloth before the elders of the city. [18] And the elders of that city shall take that _____ and _____ him; [19] And they shall amerce him in an _____ shekels of silver, and give them unto the father of the damsel, because he hath brought up an evil _____ upon a virgin of Israel: and she shall be his wife; he may not put her away all his days. [20] But if this thing be _____ , and the tokens of virginity be not found for the damsel: [21] Then they shall bring out the damsel to the door of her father's house, and the men of her city shall _____ her with stones that she _____ : because she hath wrought folly in Israel, to play the _____ in her father's _____ : so shalt thou put _____ away from among you.

[22] If a man be found _____ with a woman _____ to an husband, then they shall both of them _____ , both the man that lay with the woman, and the woman: so shalt thou put away evil from Israel.

[23] If a damsel that is a _____ be _____ unto an husband, and a man find her in the _____ , and lie with her; [24] Then ye shall bring them _____ out unto the gate of that city, and ye shall stone them with stones that they _____ ; the damsel, because she _____ _____ , being _____ the _____ ; and the _____ , because he hath _____ his neighbour's wife: so thou shalt put away evil from among you.

[25] But if a man find a _____ damsel in the _____ , and the man _____ her, and lie with her: then the _____ only that lay with her shall _____ : [26] But unto the _____ thou shalt do _____ ; there is in the damsel no sin _____ of death: for as when a man riseth against his neighbour, and slayeth him, even so is this matter: [27] For he _____ her in the _____ , and the betrothed damsel _____ , and there was _____ to save her.

[28] If a _____ find a _____ that is a _____ , which is not _____ , and lay hold on her, and _____ with her, and they be _____ ; [29] Then the man that lay with her shall give unto the damsel's father _____ shekels of silver, and she shall be his _____ ; because he hath _____ her, he may _____ put her away _____ his days.

[30] A man shall not take his father's _____ , nor discover his father's _____ .

DEUTERONOMY

[23:1] He that is _____ in the stones, or hath his privy member cut off, shall not _____ into the congregation of the Lord. [2] A bastard shall not enter into the congregation of the Lord; even to his _____ generation shall he not enter into the congregation of the Lord. [3] An Ammonite or Moabite shall not enter into the congregation of the Lord; even to their _____ generation shall they not enter into the congregation of the Lord for ever: [4] Because they met you not with bread and with water in the way, when ye came forth out of Egypt; and because they hired against thee Balaam the son of Beor of Pethor of Mesopotamia, to curse thee. [5] Nevertheless the Lord thy God would not hearken unto Balaam; but the Lord thy God turned the _____ into a _____ unto thee, because the Lord thy God loved thee. [6] Thou shalt not seek their _____ nor their _____ all thy days for ever.

[7] Thou shalt not abhor an Edomite; for he is thy brother: thou shalt not abhor an Egyptian; because thou wast a stranger in his land. [8] The children that are begotten of them shall enter into the congregation of the Lord in their _____ generation.

[9] When the host goeth forth against thine _____, then keep thee from every _____ thing.

[10] If there be among you any man, that is not _____ by reason of uncleanness that chanceth him by night, then shall he go abroad out of the camp, he shall not come within the camp: [11] But it shall be, when evening cometh on, he shall wash himself with water: and when the sun is down, he shall come into the camp again.

[12] Thou shalt have a place also without the camp, whither thou shalt go forth abroad: [13] And thou shalt have a _____ upon thy _____; and it shall be, when thou wilt ease thyself abroad, thou shalt _____ therewith, and shalt turn back and _____ that which cometh from thee: [14] For the Lord thy God _____ in the midst of thy _____, to deliver thee, and to give up thine enemies before thee; therefore shall thy camp be _____: that he see no _____ thing in thee, and _____ away from thee.

[15] Thou shalt not deliver unto his _____ the _____ which is _____ from his master unto _____: [16] He shall _____ with thee, even among you, in that _____ which he shall choose in one of thy _____, where it liketh him _____: thou shalt not _____ him.

[17] There shall be no _____ of the daughters of Israel, nor a _____ of the sons of Israel. [18] Thou shalt not bring the _____ of a _____, or the _____ of a _____, into the house of the Lord thy God for any _____: for even both these are _____ unto the Lord thy God.

[19] Thou shalt not _____ upon _____ to thy _____; usury of _____, usury of _____, usury of any _____ that is lent upon usury: [20] Unto a _____ thou _____ lend upon usury; but unto thy _____ thou shalt _____ lend upon usury: that the Lord thy God may _____ thee in all that thou settest thine hand to in the land whither thou goest to possess it.

[21] When thou shalt _____ a _____ unto the Lord thy God, thou shalt not _____ to _____ it: for the Lord thy God will surely _____ it of thee; and it would be _____ in thee. [22] But if thou shalt _____ to vow, it shall be _____ sin in thee. [23] That which is gone out of thy _____ thou shalt _____ and _____; even a _____ offering, according as thou hast _____ unto the Lord thy God, which thou hast _____ with thy mouth.

DEUTERONOMY

[24] When thou comest into thy _____ ___ vineyard, then thou mayest _____ grapes thy fill at thine own _____ ; but thou shalt not put any in thy _____ .
[25] When thou comest into the standing _____ of thy neighbour, then thou mayest _____ the ears with thine _____ ; but thou shalt _____ move a _____ unto thy neighbour's standing corn.

[24:1] When a man hath taken a _____ , and married her, and it come to pass that she find no _____ in his eyes, because he hath found some _____ in her: then let him write her a _____ of _____ , and give it in her hand, and _____ her out of his house. [2] And when she is departed out of his house, she may _____ and be _____ man's wife. [3] And if the latter husband _____ her, and write her a _____ of _____ , and giveth it in her hand, and sendeth her out of his house; or if the latter husband die, which took her to be his wife; [4] Her _____ husband, which sent her away, may _____ take her again to be his wife, after that she is _____ ; for that is _____ before the Lord: and thou shalt not cause the land to _____ , which the Lord thy God giveth thee for an inheritance.

[5] When a man hath taken a _____ wife, he shall _____ go out to _____ , neither shall he be _____ with any _____ : but he shall be _____ at home _____ year, and shall _____ up his wife which he hath taken.

[6] No man shall take the nether or the upper _____ to pledge: for he taketh a man's _____ to pledge.

[7] If a man be found _____ any of his _____ of the children of Israel, and maketh _____ of him, or _____ him; then that _____ shall _____ ; and thou shalt put evil away from among you.

[8] Take heed in the _____ of _____ , that thou observe diligently, and do according to all that the priests the Levites shall teach you: as I commanded them, so ye shall observe to do. [9] Remember what the Lord thy God did unto Miriam by the way, after that ye were come forth out of Egypt.

[10] When thou dost lend thy brother any thing, thou shalt _____ go into his house to fetch his pledge. [11] Thou shalt stand abroad, and the man to whom thou dost lend shall bring out the pledge abroad unto thee. [12] And if the man be _____ , thou shalt not _____ with his pledge: [13] In any case thou shalt _____ him the pledge again when the _____ goeth down, that he may sleep in his own raiment, and _____ thee: and it shall be righteousness unto thee before the Lord thy God.

[14] Thou shalt not oppress an hired servant that is poor and needy, whether he be of thy brethren, or of thy strangers that are in thy land within thy gates: [15] At his _____ thou shalt give him his hire, neither shall the _____ go _____ upon it; for he is _____ , and setteth his heart upon it: lest he _____ against thee unto the Lord, and it be _____ unto thee. [16] The fathers shall not be put to _____ for the _____ , neither shall the children be put to death for the fathers: every man shall be put to death for his own sin.

[17] Thou shalt not _____ the judgment of the stranger, nor of the fatherless; nor take a widow's raiment to pledge: [18] But thou shalt _____ that thou wast a

DEUTERONOMY

bondman in Egypt, and the Lord thy God redeemed thee thence: therefore I command thee to do this thing.

[19] When thou cuttest down thine harvest in thy field, and hast _____ a sheaf in the field, thou shalt _____ go again to fetch it: it shall be for the _____, for the _____, and for the _____: that the Lord thy God may _____ thee in all the work of thine hands. [20] When thou beatest thine olive tree, thou shalt not go over the boughs again: it shall be for the stranger, for the fatherless, and for the widow. [21] When thou gatherest the grapes of thy vineyard, thou shalt _____ glean it afterward: it shall be for the stranger, for the fatherless, and for the widow. [22] And thou shalt _____ that thou wast a bondman in the land of Egypt: therefore I command thee to do this thing.

[25:1] If there be a _____ between men, and they come unto judgment, that the judges may judge them; then they shall _____ the _____, and _____ the _____. [2] And it shall be, if the wicked man be worthy to be _____, that the judge shall cause him to lie down, and to be beaten before his face, according to his fault, by a certain number. [3] _____ stripes he may give him, and not _____: lest, if he should exceed, and beat him above these with many stripes, then thy brother should seem _____ unto thee.

[4] Thou shalt _____ _____ the ox when he _____ out the _____.

[5] If brethren dwell together, and one of them _____, and have no _____, the wife of the dead shall not marry without unto a stranger: her husband's _____ shall go in unto her, and take her to him to wife, and perform the _____ of an husband's brother unto her. [6] And it shall be, that the _____ which she beareth shall _____ in the _____ of his brother which is dead, that his name be not put out of Israel. [7] And if the man like not to take his brother's wife, then let his brother's wife go up to the gate unto the elders, and say, My husband's brother refuseth to raise up unto his brother a name in Israel, he will not perform the duty of my husband's brother. [8] Then the elders of his city shall call him, and speak unto him: and if he stand to it, and say, I like not to take her; [9] Then shall his brother's wife come unto him in the presence of the elders, and loose his _____ from off his foot, and _____ in his face, and shall answer and say, So shall it be done unto that man that will not build up his _____ house. [10] And his name shall be called in _____, The house of him that hath his shoe _____.

[11] When men _____ together one with another, and the _____ of the one draweth near for to _____ her husband out of the hand of him that smiteth him, and putteth forth her hand, and taketh him by the _____: [12] Then thou shalt _____ off her _____, thine eye shall not pity her.

[13] Thou shalt not have in thy bag divers _____, a great and a small. [14] Thou shalt not have in thine house divers _____, a great and a small. [15] But thou shalt have a _____ and _____ weight, a perfect and just _____ shalt thou have: that thy days may be lengthened in the land which the Lord thy God giveth thee. [16] For all that do such things, and all that do unrighteously, are an _____ unto the Lord thy God.

[17] _____ what _____ did unto thee by the way, when ye were come forth out of Egypt; [18] How he met thee by the way, and smote the hindmost of thee,

DEUTERONOMY

even all that were feeble behind thee, when thou wast faint and weary; and he _____ not God. [19] Therefore it shall be, when the Lord thy God hath given thee rest from all thine enemies round about, in the land which the Lord thy God giveth thee for an inheritance to possess it, that thou shalt _____ out the _____ of Amalek from under heaven; thou shalt not forget it.

[26:1] And it shall be, when thou art come in unto the land which the Lord thy God giveth thee for an inheritance, and possessest it, and dwellest therein; [2] That thou shalt take of the _____ of all the _____ of the earth, which thou shalt bring of thy land that the Lord thy God giveth thee, and shalt put it in a _____ , and shalt go unto the place which the Lord thy God shall choose to place his name there. [3] And thou shalt go unto the priest that shall be in those days, and say unto him, I profess this day unto the Lord thy God, that I am come unto the country which the Lord sware unto our fathers for to give us. [4] And the _____ shall take the basket out of thine hand, and set it down before the _____ of the Lord thy God. [5] And thou shalt speak and say before the Lord thy God, A _____ ready to _____ was my father, and he went down into _____ , and _____ there with a few, and became there a nation, great, mighty, and populous: [6] And the Egyptians evil entreated us, and afflicted us, and laid upon us hard bondage: [7] And when we _____ unto the Lord God of our fathers, the Lord heard our voice, and looked on our _____ , and our labour, and our oppression: [8] And the Lord brought us forth out of Egypt with a _____ hand, and with an outstretched arm, and with great terribleness, and with signs, and with wonders: [9] And he hath brought us into this place, and hath given us this land, even a land that floweth with _____ and _____ . [10] And now, behold, I have brought the _____ of the land, which thou, O Lord, hast given me. And thou shalt set it before the Lord thy God, and _____ before the Lord thy God: [11] And thou shalt _____ in every _____ thing which the Lord thy God hath given unto _____ , and unto thine _____ , thou, and the Levite, and the stranger that is among you.

[12] When thou hast made an end of _____ all the tithes of thine _____ the third year, which is the year of tithing, and hast given it unto the _____ , the _____ , the _____ , and the _____ , that they may eat within thy gates, and be filled; [13] Then thou shalt say before the Lord thy God, I have brought away the _____ things out of mine house, and also have _____ them unto the Levite, and unto the stranger, to the fatherless, and to the widow, according to all thy commandments which thou hast commanded me: I have _____ transgressed thy commandments, neither have I _____ them: [14] I have not eaten thereof in my mourning, neither have I taken away ought thereof for any unclean use, nor given ought thereof for the dead: but I have _____ to the _____ of the _____ my God, and have done according to all that thou hast commanded me. [15] Look down from thy _____ habitation, from _____ , and _____ thy people Israel, and the land which thou hast given us, as thou swarest unto our fathers, a land that floweth with _____ and _____ .

[16] This day the Lord thy God hath commanded thee to do these statutes and judgments: thou shalt therefore keep and do them with _____ thine _____ , and with all thy _____ . [17] Thou hast _____ the Lord this day to be thy God, and to walk in his ways, and to keep his statutes, and his commandments, and his

DEUTERONOMY

judgments, and to hearken unto his voice: [18] And the Lord hath _____ thee this day to be his _____ people, as he hath promised thee, and that thou shouldest keep all his commandments; [19] And to make thee high above all nations which he hath made, in _____ , and in name, and in _____ ; and that thou mayest be an _____ people unto the Lord thy God, as he hath spoken.

[27:1] And Moses with the elders of Israel commanded the people, saying, _____ all the commandments which I command you this day. [2] And it shall be on the day when ye shall pass over Jordan unto the land which the Lord thy God giveth thee, that thou shalt set thee up great _____ , and _____ them with plaister: [3] And thou shalt _____ upon them all the _____ of this law, when thou art passed over, that thou mayest go in unto the land which the Lord thy God giveth thee, a land that floweth with milk and honey; as the Lord God of thy fathers hath promised thee. [4] Therefore it shall be when ye be gone over Jordan, that ye shall set up these stones, which I command you this day, in mount Ebal, and thou shalt plaister them with plaister. [5] And there shalt thou build an _____ unto the Lord thy God, an altar of _____ : thou shalt not lift up any iron tool upon them. [6] Thou shalt build the altar of the Lord thy God of _____ stones: and thou shalt offer burnt offerings thereon unto the Lord thy God: [7] And thou shalt offer peace offerings, and shalt eat there, and rejoice before the Lord thy God. [8] And thou shalt _____ upon the _____ all the _____ of this law very _____ .

[9] And Moses and the priests the Levites spake unto all Israel, saying, Take heed, and hearken, O Israel; this day thou art _____ the people of the Lord thy God. [10] Thou shalt therefore _____ the _____ of the Lord thy God, and do his commandments and his statutes, which I command thee this day.

[11] And Moses charged the people the same day, saying, [12] These shall stand upon mount Gerizim to _____ the people, when ye are come over Jordan; Simeon, and Levi, and Judah, and Issachar, and Joseph, and Benjamin: [13] And these shall stand upon mount Ebal to curse; Reuben, Gad, and Asher, and Zebulun, Dan, and Naphtali.

[14] And the Levites shall speak, and say unto all the men of Israel with a loud voice, [15] _____ be the man that maketh any _____ or molten _____ , an abomination unto the Lord, the work of the hands of the craftsman, and putteth it in a _____ place. And all the people shall answer and say, _____ . [16] _____ be he that setteth _____ by his _____ or his _____ . And all the people shall say, _____ . [17] _____ be he that _____ his neighbour's _____ . And all the people shall say, _____ . [18] _____ be he that maketh the _____ to wander out of the way. And all the people shall say, _____ . [19] _____ be he that _____ the judgment of the stranger, fatherless, and widow. And all the people shall say, _____ . [20] Cursed be he that lieth with his father's wife; because he uncovereth his father's skirt. And all the people shall say, _____ . [21] _____ be he that _____ with any manner of _____ . And all the people shall say, _____ . [22] _____ be he that _____ with his _____ , the daughter of his father, or the daughter of his mother. And all the people shall say, _____ . [23] _____ be he that _____ with his _____ in _____ . And all the people shall say, _____ . [24] _____ be he that smiteth his neighbour _____ . And all the people shall say, _____ . [25] _____ be he that taketh _____ to

DEUTERONOMY

_____ an innocent person. And all the people shall say, _____ . [26] _____ be he that _____ not all the _____ of this law to _____ them. And all the people shall say, _____ .

[28:1] And it shall come to pass, if thou shalt hearken diligently unto the voice of the Lord thy God, to observe and to do all his commandments which I command thee this day, that the Lord thy God will set thee on high above all nations of the earth: [2] And all these _____ shall come on thee, and _____ thee, if thou shalt hearken unto the voice of the Lord thy God. [3] _____ shalt thou be in the _____ , and _____ shalt thou be in the _____ . [4] _____ shall be the _____ of thy _____ , and the _____ of thy _____ , and the _____ of thy _____ , the _____ of thy _____ , and the _____ of thy _____ . [5] _____ shall be thy _____ and thy _____ . [6] _____ shalt thou be when thou _____ in, and _____ shalt thou be when thou goest _____ . [7] The Lord shall cause thine enemies that rise up against thee to be smitten before thy face: they shall come out against thee _____ way, and flee before thee _____ ways. [8] The Lord shall _____ the _____ upon thee in thy _____ , and in all that thou _____ thine _____ unto; and he shall _____ thee in the _____ which the Lord thy God giveth thee. [9] The Lord shall _____ thee an holy people unto himself, as he hath sworn unto thee, if thou shalt keep the commandments of the Lord thy God, and walk in his ways. [10] And all people of the earth shall _____ that thou art called by the name of the Lord; and they shall be _____ of thee. [11] And the Lord shall make thee plenteous in _____ , in the fruit of thy body, and in the fruit of thy cattle, and in the fruit of thy ground, in the land which the Lord sware unto thy fathers to give thee. [12] The Lord shall open unto thee his good _____ , the heaven to give the _____ unto thy land in his season, and to _____ all the work of thine hand: and thou shalt _____ unto many nations, and thou shalt not _____ . [13] And the Lord shall _____ thee the _____ , and not the _____ ; and thou shalt be _____ only, and thou shalt not be _____ ; if that thou hearken unto the commandments of the Lord thy God, which I command thee this day, to observe and to do them: [14] And thou shalt _____ go _____ from any of the words which I command thee this day, to the _____ hand, or to the _____ , to go after other _____ to serve them.

[15] But it shall come to pass, if thou wilt _____ hearken unto the voice of the Lord thy God, to observe to do all his commandments and his statutes which I command thee this day; that all these _____ shall come upon thee, and _____ thee: [16] _____ shalt thou be in the _____ , and _____ shalt thou be in the _____ . [17] _____ shall be thy basket and thy _____ . [18] _____ shall be the _____ of thy _____ , and the _____ of thy _____ , the increase of thy kine, and the flocks of thy sheep. [19] _____ shalt thou be when thou comest _____ , and _____ shalt thou be when thou goest _____ . [20] The Lord shall send upon thee _____ , _____ , and _____ , in all that thou _____ thine _____ unto for to do, until thou be destroyed, and until thou _____ quickly; because of the _____ of thy doings, whereby thou hast forsaken me. [21] The Lord shall make the _____ cleave unto thee, until he have consumed thee from off the land, whither thou goest to possess it. [22]

DEUTERONOMY

The Lord shall smite thee with a _____ , and with a _____ , and with an _____ , and with an extreme burning, and with the _____ , and with _____ , and with _____ ; and they shall pursue thee until thou _____ . [23] And thy _____ that is over thy head shall be _____ , and the _____ that is under thee shall be _____ . [24] The Lord shall make the _____ of thy land _____ and _____ : from heaven shall it come down upon thee, until thou be _____ .

[25] The Lord shall cause thee to be _____ before thine enemies: thou shalt go out _____ way against them, and flee _____ ways before them: and shalt be removed into all the kingdoms of the earth. [26] And thy carcase shall be meat unto all fowls of the air, and unto the beasts of the earth, and no man shall _____ them away. [27] The Lord will smite thee with the _____ of Egypt, and with the _____ , and with the _____ , and with the _____ , whereof thou canst _____ be _____ . [28] The Lord shall smite thee with _____ , and _____ , and _____ of _____ : [29] And thou shalt _____ at _____ , as the blind gropeth in darkness, and thou shalt _____ prosper in thy ways: and thou shalt be only _____ and spoiled evermore, and _____ man shall _____ thee. [30] Thou shalt betroth a _____ , and another man shall _____ with her: thou shalt build an _____ , and thou shalt not dwell therein: thou shalt plant a _____ , and shalt _____ gather the grapes thereof. [31] Thine ox shall be slain before thine eyes, and thou shalt not eat thereof: thine ass shall be _____ taken away from before thy face, and shall not be _____ to thee: thy sheep shall be given unto thine enemies, and thou shalt have _____ to rescue them. [32] Thy sons and thy daughters shall be _____ unto another _____ , and thine eyes shall _____ , and fail with _____ for them all the day long: and there shall be no _____ in thine hand. [33] The fruit of thy land, and all thy labours, shall a nation which thou knowest not eat up; and thou shalt be only oppressed and _____ alway: [34] So that thou shalt be _____ for the sight of thine eyes which thou shalt see. [35] The Lord shall smite thee in the _____ , and in the _____ , with a sore botch that cannot be healed, from the sole of thy _____ unto the top of thy _____ .

[36] The Lord shall bring thee, and thy _____ which thou shalt set over thee, unto a nation which neither thou nor thy fathers have known; and there shalt thou serve other gods, wood and stone. [37] And thou shalt become an _____ , a _____ , and a _____ , among all nations whither the Lord shall lead thee. [38] Thou shalt carry much seed out into the field, and shalt gather but little in; for the locust shall consume it. [39] Thou shalt plant vineyards, and dress them, but shalt neither drink of the wine, nor gather the grapes; for the worms shall eat them. [40] Thou shalt have olive trees throughout all thy coasts, but thou shalt not anoint thyself with the oil; for thine olive shall cast his fruit. [41] Thou shalt beget sons and daughters, but thou shalt not enjoy them; for they shall go into captivity. [42] All thy trees and fruit of thy land shall the locust consume. [43] The stranger that is within thee shall get up above thee very high; and thou shalt come down very low. [44] He shall _____ to thee, and thou shalt not _____ to him: he shall be the _____ , and thou shalt be the _____ .

[45] Moreover all these _____ shall come upon thee, and shall _____ thee, and _____ thee, till thou be _____ ; because thou hearkenedst not unto the

DEUTERONOMY

voice of the Lord thy God, to keep his commandments and his statutes which he commanded thee: [46] And they shall be upon thee for a _____ and for a _____, and upon thy _____ for ever. [47] Because thou _____ not the Lord thy God with _____, and with _____ of heart, for the _____ of all _____; [48] Therefore shalt thou _____ thine _____ which the Lord shall send against thee, in _____, and in _____, and in _____, and in _____ of all things: and he shall put a _____ of iron upon thy neck, until he have _____ thee. [49] The Lord shall bring a _____ against thee from far, from the end of the earth, as _____ as the _____ flieth; a nation whose _____ thou shalt not understand; [50] A nation of _____ countenance, which shall not regard the person of the _____, nor shew favour to the _____: [51] And he shall _____ the fruit of thy cattle, and the fruit of thy land, until thou be _____: which also shall not leave thee either _____, wine, or oil, or the increase of thy kine, or flocks of thy sheep, until he have destroyed thee. [52] And he shall _____ thee in all thy gates, until thy high and fenced walls come down, wherein thou trustedst, throughout all thy land: and he shall besiege thee in all thy gates throughout all thy land, which the Lord thy God hath given thee. [53] And thou shalt eat the fruit of thine own body, the flesh of thy sons and of thy daughters, which the Lord thy God hath given thee, in the siege, and in the straitness, wherewith thine enemies shall distress thee: [54] So that the _____ that is _____ among you, and very _____, his eye shall be evil toward his brother, and toward the wife of his bosom, and toward the remnant of his children which he shall leave: [55] So that he will not give to any of them of the flesh of his children whom he shall _____: because he hath nothing left him in the siege, and in the straitness, wherewith thine enemies shall distress thee in all thy gates. [56] The _____ and _____ woman among you, which would not adventure to set the sole of her foot upon the ground for delicateness and tenderness, her eye shall be _____ toward the _____ of her bosom, and toward her _____, and toward her _____, [57] And toward her young one that cometh out from between her feet, and toward her children which she shall bear: for she shall _____ them for want of all things secretly in the siege and straitness, wherewith thine enemy shall distress thee in thy gates. [58] If thou wilt not observe to do all the words of this law that are written in this book, that thou mayest _____ this _____ and _____ _____, _____ _____ _____ _____; [59] Then the Lord will make thy plagues wonderful, and the plagues of thy seed, even great plagues, and of long _____, and sore _____, and of long _____. [60] Moreover he will bring upon thee all the diseases of Egypt, which thou wast afraid of; and they shall cleave unto thee. [61] Also every _____, and every plague, which is not written in the book of this law, them will the Lord bring upon thee, until thou be destroyed. [62] And ye shall be left _____ in number, whereas ye were as the _____ of heaven for multitude; because thou wouldest not obey the voice of the Lord thy God. [63] And it shall come to pass, that as the Lord _____ over you to do you _____, and to multiply you; so the Lord will _____ over you to _____ you, and to bring you to nought; and ye shall be plucked from off the land whither thou goest to possess it. [64] And the Lord shall _____ thee among all people, from the one end of the earth even unto the other; and there thou shalt _____ other _____, which neither

DEUTERONOMY

thou nor thy fathers have known, even wood and stone. [65] And among these nations shalt thou find no _____ , neither shall the sole of thy foot have _____ : but the Lord shall give thee there a _____ heart, and _____ of eyes, and _____ of mind: [66] And thy _____ shall hang in _____ before thee; and thou shalt _____ day and night, and shalt have none _____ of thy _____ : [67] In the morning thou shalt say, Would God it were even! and at even thou shalt say, Would God it were morning! for the fear of thine heart wherewith thou shalt fear, and for the sight of thine eyes which thou shalt see. [68] And the Lord shall bring thee into Egypt again with ships, by the way whereof I spake unto thee, Thou shalt see it no more again: and there ye shall be sold unto your enemies for bondmen and bondwomen, and no man shall buy you.

[29:1] These are the words of the _____ , which the Lord commanded Moses to make with the children of Israel in the land of _____ , _____ the _____ which he made with them in _____ .

[2] And Moses called unto all Israel, and said unto them, Ye have seen all that the Lord did before your eyes in the land of Egypt unto Pharaoh, and unto all his servants, and unto all his land; [3] The great temptations which thine eyes have seen, the signs, and those great miracles: [4] Yet the Lord hath not given you an heart to perceive, and eyes to see, and ears to hear, unto this day. [5] And I have led you _____ years in the _____ : your _____ are not waxen _____ upon you, and thy _____ is not waxen _____ upon thy foot. [6] Ye have not eaten _____ , neither have ye drunk _____ or strong _____ : that ye might know that I am the Lord your God. [7] And when ye came unto this place, _____ the king of _____ , and _____ the king of _____ , came out against us unto battle, and we smote them: [8] And we took their land, and gave it for an inheritance unto the Reubenites, and to the Gadites, and to the half tribe of Manasseh. [9] Keep therefore the words of this covenant, and do them, that ye may _____ in all that _____ do.

[10] Ye stand this day all of you before the Lord your God; your captains of your tribes, your elders, and your officers, with all the men of Israel, [11] Your little ones, your wives, and thy stranger that is in thy camp, from the hewer of thy wood unto the drawer of thy water: [12] That thou shouldest enter into covenant with the Lord thy God, and into his oath, which the Lord thy God maketh with thee this day: [13] That he may establish thee to day for a people unto himself, and that he may be unto thee a God, as he hath said unto thee, and as he hath sworn unto thy fathers, to _____ , to _____ , and to _____ . [14] Neither with you _____ do I make this covenant and this oath; [15] But with him that _____ here _____ _____ this day before the Lord our God, and also with _____ that is not _____ with us this day: [16] (For ye know how we have dwelt in the land of Egypt; and how we came through the nations which ye passed by; [17] And ye have seen their abominations, and their idols, wood and stone, silver and gold, which were among them:) [18] Lest there should be among you man, or woman, or family, or tribe, whose heart turneth away this day from the Lord our God, to go and serve the gods of these nations; lest there should be among you a _____ that beareth _____ and _____ ; [19] And it come to pass, when he heareth the words of this curse, that he bless himself in his heart, saying, I shall have _____ , though I _____ in the _____ of mine _____ , to add _____ to thirst: [20] The Lord will not _____

DEUTERONOMY

him, but then the _____ of the Lord and his _____ shall smoke against that man, and all the _____ that are written in this book shall lie upon him, and the Lord shall blot out his name from under heaven. [21] And the Lord shall separate him unto evil out of all the tribes of Israel, according to all the curses of the covenant that are written in this book of the law: [22] So that the generation to come of your children that shall rise up after you, and the stranger that shall come from a far land, shall say, when they see the plagues of that land, and the sicknesses which the Lord hath laid upon it; [23] And that the whole land thereof is _____ , and _____ , and _____ , that it is _____ sown, nor _____ , nor any _____ groweth therein, like the overthrow of _____ , and _____ , _____ , and _____ , which the Lord overthrew in his _____ , and in his _____ : [24] Even all nations shall say, Wherefore hath the Lord done thus unto this land? what meaneth the _____ of this great anger? [25] Then men shall say, Because they have forsaken the covenant of the Lord God of their fathers, which he made with them when he brought them forth out of the land of Egypt: [26] For they went and served other gods, and worshipped them, gods whom they knew not, and whom he had not given unto them: [27] And the anger of the Lord was kindled against this land, to bring upon it all the curses that are written in this book: [28] And the Lord rooted them out of their land in anger, and in wrath, and in great indignation, and cast them into another land, as it is this day. [29] The _____ _____ belong unto the _____ our God: but those things which are _____ belong unto _____ and to our _____ for ever, that we may do _____ the _____ of this _____ .

[30:1] And it shall come to pass, when all these things are come upon thee, the _____ and the _____ , which I have set before thee, and thou shalt call them to mind among all the nations, whither the Lord thy God hath driven thee, [2] And shalt return unto the Lord thy God, and shalt _____ his voice according to all that I command thee this day, thou and thy children, with all thine _____ , and with all thy _____ ; [3] That then the Lord thy God will turn thy captivity, and have compassion upon thee, and will return and gather thee from all the nations, whither the Lord thy God hath scattered thee. [4] If any of thine be driven out unto the outmost parts of heaven, from thence will the Lord thy God _____ thee, and from thence will he _____ thee: [5] And the Lord thy God will bring thee into the land which thy fathers possessed, and thou shalt possess it; and he will do thee good, and multiply thee above thy fathers. [6] And the Lord thy God will circumcise thine heart, and the heart of thy seed, to love the Lord thy God with all thine heart, and with all thy soul, that thou mayest live. [7] And the Lord thy God will put all these curses upon thine enemies, and on them that hate thee, which persecuted thee. [8] And thou shalt return and obey the voice of the Lord, and do all his commandments which I command thee this day. [9] And the Lord thy God will make thee plenteous in every work of thine hand, in the fruit of thy body, and in the fruit of thy cattle, and in the fruit of thy land, for good: for the Lord will again rejoice over thee for good, as he rejoiced over thy fathers: [10] If thou shalt hearken unto the voice of the Lord thy God, to keep his commandments and his statutes which are written in this book of the law, and if thou turn unto the Lord thy God with all thine heart, and with all thy soul.

[11] For this _____ which I command thee this day, it is not _____ from thee, _____ is it _____ off. [12] It is not in _____ , that thou shouldest

DEUTERONOMY

say, Who shall go up for us to heaven, and bring it unto us, that we may _____ it, and do it? [13] Neither is it _____ the _____ , that thou shouldest say, Who shall go over the sea for us, and bring it unto us, that we may hear it, and do it? [14] But the _____ is very _____ unto thee, in thy _____ , and in thy _____ , that _____ mayest _____ it.

[15] See, I have set before thee this day _____ and _____ , and _____ and _____ ; [16] In that I _____ thee this day to _____ the _____ thy _____ , to _____ in his _____ , and to _____ his _____ and his _____ and his _____ , that thou mayest _____ and _____ : and the Lord thy God shall _____ thee in the land whither thou goest to _____ it. [17] But if thine heart _____ _____ away, so that thou wilt not _____ , but shalt be _____ away, and _____ other _____ , and _____ them; [18] I _____ unto you this day, that ye shall surely _____ , and that ye shall _____ prolong your days upon the land, whither thou passest over Jordan to go to possess it. [19] I call _____ and _____ to _____ this day against you, that I have _____ before you _____ and _____ , _____ and _____ : therefore choose _____ , that both thou and thy seed may _____ : [20] That thou mayest _____ the _____ thy God, and that thou mayest _____ his voice, and that thou mayest _____ unto _____ : for _____ is thy _____ , and the length of thy days: that thou mayest dwell in the land which the Lord sware unto thy fathers, to Abraham, to Isaac, and to Jacob, to give them.

[31:1] And Moses went and spake these words unto all Israel. [2] And he said unto them, I am an _____ and _____ years old _____ _____ ; I can no more go out and come in: also the Lord hath said unto me, Thou shalt _____ go over this Jordan. [3] The Lord thy God, he will go over before thee, and he will destroy these nations from before thee, and thou shalt possess them: and _____ , he shall go over before thee, as the Lord hath said. [4] And the Lord shall do unto them as he did to _____ and to _____ , kings of the _____ , and unto the land of them, whom he destroyed. [5] And the Lord shall give them up before your face, that ye may do unto them according unto all the commandments which I have commanded you. [6] Be _____ and of a good _____ , _____ not, nor be _____ of them: for the _____ thy God, he it is that doth go _____ thee; he will _____ _____ thee, nor _____ thee.

[7] And _____ called unto _____ , and said unto him in the _____ of all Israel, Be _____ and of a _____ _____ : for thou must go with this people unto the land which the Lord hath sworn unto their fathers to give them; and thou shalt cause them to inherit it. [8] And the Lord, he it is that doth go before thee; he will be with thee, he will not fail thee, neither forsake thee: _____ not, neither be disma_____ ed.

[9] And Moses _____ this _____ , and delivered it unto the priests the sons of Levi, which bare the _____ of the covenant of the Lord, and unto all the _____ of Israel. [10] And Moses commanded them, saying, At the end of every _____ years, in the solemnity of the year of release, in the feast of _____ , [11] When all Israel is come to appear before the Lord thy God in the place which he shall choose, thou shalt _____ this law before all Israel in their hearing. [12] Gather

DEUTERONOMY

the people together, _____ , and _____ , and _____ , and thy _____ that is within thy gates, that they may _____ , and that they may _____ , and _____ the Lord your God, and _____ to do all the words of this law: [13] And that their _____ , which have not _____ any thing, may _____ , and _____ to _____ the Lord your God, as long as ye live in the land whither ye go over Jordan to possess it.

[14] And the Lord said unto Moses, Behold, thy days approach that thou must _____ : call _____ , and present yourselves in the _____ of the congregation, that I may give him a _____ . And _____ and _____ went, and _____ themselves in the _____ of the congregation. [15] And the Lord _____ in the tabernacle in a _____ of a _____ : and the _____ of the _____ stood _____ the _____ of the tabernacle.

[16] And the Lord said unto Moses, Behold, thou shalt _____ with thy fathers; and this people will rise up, and go a whoring after the gods of the strangers of the land, whither they go to be among them, and will _____ me, and _____ my _____ which I have made with them. [17] Then my _____ shall be kindled against them in that day, and I will forsake them, and I will hide my face from them, and they shall be devoured, and many evils and troubles shall befall them; so that they will say in that day, Are not these evils come upon us, because our God is not among us? [18] And I will surely hide my face in that day for all the evils which they shall have wrought, in that they are turned unto other gods. [19] Now therefore _____ ye this _____ for you, and teach it the children of Israel: put it in their mouths, that this song may be a witness for me against the children of Israel. [20] For when I shall have brought them into the land which I sware unto their fathers, that floweth with milk and honey; and they shall have eaten and filled themselves, and waxen fat; then will they turn unto other gods, and serve them, and provoke me, and break my covenant. [21] And it shall come to pass, when many evils and troubles are befallen them, that this _____ shall _____ against them as a _____ ; for it shall not be forgotten out of the mouths of their seed: for I know their imagination which they go about, even now, before I have brought them into the land which I sware.

[22] _____ therefore _____ this _____ the same day, and _____ it the children of Israel. [23] And he gave _____ the son of _____ a _____ , and said, Be _____ and of a _____ _____ : for thou shalt bring the children of Israel into the land which I sware unto them: and I will be with thee.

[24] And it came to pass, when Moses had made an end of writing the words of this law in a book, until they were finished, [25] That Moses commanded the Levites, which bare the ark of the covenant of the Lord, saying, [26] Take this _____ of the _____ , and put it in the _____ of the _____ of the covenant of the Lord your God, that it may be there for a witness against thee. [27] For I know thy _____ , and thy stiff neck: behold, while I am yet _____ with you this day, ye have been _____ against the Lord; and how much more after my death?

[28] Gather unto me all the elders of your tribes, and your officers, that I may speak these words in their ears, and call heaven and earth to _____ against them. [29] For I know that after my death ye will utterly corrupt yourselves, and turn aside from the way which I have commanded you; and evil will befall you in the latter days; because ye will

DEUTERONOMY

do evil in the sight of the Lord, to provoke him to anger through the work of your hands. [30] And Moses spake in the ears of all the congregation of Israel the words of this song, until they were ended.

[32:1] Give _____ , O ye heavens, and I will speak; and _____ , O earth, the words of my mouth. [2] My _____ shall drop as the rain, my speech shall distil as the dew, as the small rain upon the tender herb, and as the showers upon the grass: [3] Because I will _____ the name of the _____ : ascribe ye _____ unto our God. [4] He is the _____ , his work is _____ : for all his ways are judgment: a God of _____ and without iniquity, just and _____ is he. [5] They have corrupted themselves, their spot is not the spot of his children: they are a perverse and crooked generation. [6] Do ye thus requite the Lord, O foolish people and unwise? is not he thy father that hath bought thee? hath he not made thee, and established thee?

[7] _____ the days of _____ , consider the years of many generations: ask thy father, and he will _____ thee; thy elders, and they will _____ thee. [8] When the most High divided to the nations their inheritance, when he separated the sons of Adam, he set the _____ of the people according to the number of the children of Israel. [9] For the Lord's _____ is his people; Jacob is the lot of his inheritance. [10] He found him in a desert land, and in the waste howling wilderness; he led him about, he instructed him, he kept him as the _____ of his eye. [11] As an _____ stirreth up her _____ , _____ over her young, _____ abroad her _____ , taketh them, _____ them on her _____ : [12] So the Lord alone did _____ him, and there was no strange god with him. [13] He made him _____ on the _____ places of the earth, that he might eat the increase of the fields; and he made him to suck honey out of the rock, and oil out of the flinty rock; [14] Butter of kine, and milk of sheep, with fat of lambs, and rams of the breed of Bashan, and goats, with the fat of kidneys of wheat; and thou didst drink the pure blood of the grape.

[15] But _____ waxed fat, and kicked: thou art waxen fat, thou art grown thick, thou art covered with fatness; then he forsook God which made him, and lightly esteemed the _____ of his _____ . [16] They provoked him to jealousy with strange gods, with abominations provoked they him to anger. [17] They sacrificed unto devils, not to God; to gods whom they knew not, to new gods that came newly up, whom your fathers feared not. [18] Of the _____ that begat thee thou art _____ , and hast _____ God that _____ thee. [19] And when the Lord saw it, he abhorred them, because of the provoking of his sons, and of his daughters. [20] And he said, I will hide my face from them, I will see what their end shall be: for they are a very froward generation, children in whom is no _____ . [21] They have moved me to _____ with that which is not God; they have provoked me to anger with their vanities: and I will move them to jealousy with those which are not a people; I will provoke them to anger with a foolish nation. [22] For a fire is kindled in mine anger, and shall burn unto the lowest _____ , and shall consume the earth with her increase, and set on fire the foundations of the mountains. [23] I will heap mischiefs upon them; I will spend mine arrows upon them. [24] They shall be burnt with hunger, and devoured with burning heat, and with bitter destruction: I will also send the teeth of beasts upon them, with the poison of serpents of the dust. [25] The _____ without, and

DEUTERONOMY

_____ within, shall destroy both the young man and the virgin, the suckling also with the man of gray hairs. [26] I said, I would scatter them into corners, I would make the remembrance of them to cease from among men: [27] Were it not that I feared the wrath of the enemy, lest their adversaries should behave themselves strangely, and lest they should say, Our hand is high, and the Lord hath not done all this. [28] For they are a nation void of counsel, neither is there any understanding in them. [29] O that they were wise, that they understood this, that they would consider their latter end! [30] How should _____ chase a _____ , and _____ put _____ _____ to flight, except their _____ had sold them, and the _____ had shut them up? [31] For their _____ is not as our _____ , even our enemies themselves being judges. [32] For their _____ is of the _____ of _____ , and of the fields of _____ : their _____ are grapes of _____ , their _____ are _____ : [33] Their _____ is the pois_____ n of dragons, and the cruel _____ of asps. [34] Is not this laid up in store with me, and sealed up among my treasures? [35] To me belongeth vengeance, and recompence; their foot shall slide in due time: for the day of their calamity is at hand, and the things that shall come upon them make haste. [36] For the Lord shall judge his people, and repent himself for his servants, when he seeth that their power is gone, and there is none shut up, or left. [37] And he shall say, Where are their gods, their rock in whom they trusted, [38] Which did eat the fat of their sacrifices, and drank the wine of their drink offerings? let them rise up and help you, and be your protection. [39] See now that I, even I, am he, and there is no _____ with me: I _____ , and I make _____ ; I _____ , and I _____ : neither is there any that can _____ out of my hand. [40] For I lift up my hand to heaven, and say, I _____ for _____ . [41] If I whet my glittering _____ , and mine hand take hold on _____ ; I will render vengeance to mine enemies, and will reward them that hate me. [42] I will make mine arrows drunk with _____ , and my sword shall devour _____ ; and that with the _____ of the slain and of the captives, from the beginning of revenges upon the enemy. [43] Rejoice, O ye nations, with his people: for he will avenge the blood of his servants, and will render vengeance to his adversaries, and will be _____ unto his land, and to his _____ .

   [44] And _____ came and spake all the words of this song in the ears of the people, he, and _____ the son of Nun. [45] And Moses made an end of speaking all these words to all Israel: [46] And he said unto them, _____ your _____ unto all the words which I testify among you this day, which ye shall _____ your _____ to _____ to do, all the words of this law. [47] For it is not a _____ thing for you; because it is your _____ : and through this thing ye shall prolong your days in the land, whither ye go over Jordan to possess it. [48] And the Lord spake unto Moses that selfsame day, saying, [49] Get thee up into this mountain _____ , unto mount _____ , which is in the land of Moab, that is over against Jericho; and _____ the land of _____ , which I give unto the children of Israel for a possession: [50] And _____ in the mount whither thou goest up, and be gathered unto thy people; as Aaron thy brother died in mount Hor, and was gathered unto his people: [51] Because ye _____ against me among the children of Israel at the waters of Meribah-Kadesh, in the wilderness of Zin; because ye _____ me _____ in the midst of the children of Israel. [52] Yet thou shalt _____ the

DEUTERONOMY

land before thee; but thou shalt _____ go thither unto the land which I give the children of Israel.

[33:1] And this is the _____, wherewith Moses the man of God blessed the children of Israel before his death. [2] And he said, The Lord came from Sinai, and rose up from Seir unto them; he shined forth from mount Paran, and he came with ten thousands of saints: from his right hand went a fiery law for them. [3] Yea, he _____ the people; all his saints are in thy hand: and they sat down at thy feet; every one shall receive of thy words. [4] Moses commanded us a law, even the inheritance of the congregation of Jacob. [5] And he was king in Jeshurun, when the heads of the people and the tribes of Israel were gathered together.

[6] Let _____ _____, and not die; and let not his men be few.

[7] And this is the _____ of _____ : and he said, Hear, Lord, the voice of Judah, and bring him unto his people: let his _____ be _____ for him; and be thou an _____ to him from his enemies. [8] And of _____ he said, Let thy Thummim and thy Urim be with thy _____ one, whom thou didst prove at Massah, and with whom thou didst strive at the waters of Meribah; [9] Who said unto his father and to his mother, I have not seen him; neither did he acknowledge his brethren, nor knew his own children: for they have observed thy word, and kept thy covenant. [10] They shall teach Jacob thy judgments, and Israel thy law: they shall put incense before thee, and whole burnt sacrifice upon thine altar. [11] _____, Lord, his _____, and accept the _____ of his hands: smite through the loins of them that rise against him, and of them that hate him, that they rise not again.

[12] And of _____ he said, The beloved of the Lord shall _____ in _____ by him; and the Lord shall _____ him all the day long, and he shall dwell between his shoulders.

[13] And of _____ he said, _____ of the Lord be his _____, for the precious things of heaven, for the dew, and for the deep that coucheth beneath, [14] And for the precious fruits brought forth by the sun, and for the precious things put forth by the moon, [15] And for the chief things of the ancient mountains, and for the precious things of the lasting hills, [16] And for the precious things of the earth and fulness thereof, and for the good will of him that dwelt in the bush: let the blessing come upon the head of Joseph, and upon the top of the head of him that was separated from his brethren. [17] His glory is like the firstling of his bullock, and his horns are like the horns of unicorns: with them he shall push the people together to the ends of the earth: and they are the _____ thousands of _____, and they are the _____ of _____.

[18] And of _____ he said, Rejoice, Zebulun, in thy going _____; and, _____, in thy _____. [19] They shall call the people unto the mountain; there they shall offer sacrifices of righteousness: for they shall suck of the abundance of the seas, and of _____ hid in the _____.

[20] And of _____ he said, _____ be he that _____ Gad: he dwelleth as a _____, and _____ the arm with the crown of the head. [21] And he provided the first part for himself, because there, in a portion of the _____, was he seated; and he came with the heads of the people, he executed the _____ of the Lord, and his judgments with Israel.

[22] And of Dan he said, Dan is a lion's whelp: he shall leap from Bashan.

DEUTERONOMY

[23] And of _____ he said, O _____ , satisfied with _____ , and full with the _____ of the Lord: possess thou the _____ and the _____ .

[24] And of _____ he said, Let Asher be _____ with _____ ; let him be _____ to his brethren, and let him dip his foot in _____ . [25] Thy shoes shall be _____ and _____ ; and as thy _____ , so shall thy _____ be.

[26] There is none like unto the God of _____ , who rideth upon the _____ in thy _____ , and in his excellency on the sky. [27] The _____ God is thy _____ , and underneath are the everlasting _____ : and he shall thrust out the enemy from before thee; and shall say, _____ them. [28] Israel then shall dwell in safety alone: the fountain of Jacob shall be upon a land of corn and wine; also his heavens shall drop down dew. [29] _____ art thou, O Israel: who is like unto thee, O people _____ by the Lord, the shield of thy help, and who is the sword of thy excellency! and thine enemies shall be found _____ unto thee; and thou shalt tread upon their high places.

[34:1] And _____ went up from the plains of Moab unto the mountain of _____ , to the top of _____ , that is over against _____ . And the Lord shewed him all the land of Gilead, unto Dan, [2] And all Naphtali, and the land of Ephraim, and Manasseh, and all the land of Judah, unto the utmost sea, [3] And the south, and the plain of the valley of Jericho, the city of palm trees, unto Zoar. [4] And the Lord said unto him, _____ is the _____ which I sware unto _____ , unto _____ , and unto _____ , saying, I will give it unto thy seed: I have caused thee to _____ it with thine eyes, but thou shalt not go over thither.

[5] So _____ the _____ of the Lord _____ there in the land of Moab, according to the word of the Lord. [6] And _____ buried him in a valley in the land of Moab, over against Beth-peor: but _____ man _____ of his sepulchre unto this day.

[7] And Moses was an _____ and _____ years old when he died: his _____ was not _____ , nor his _____ force _____ .

[8] And the children of Israel _____ for Moses in the plains of Moab _____ days: so the days of weeping and mourning for Moses were ended.

[9] And _____ the son of Nun was full of the _____ of _____ ; for Moses had laid his _____ upon him: and the children of Israel _____ unto him, and did as the Lord commanded Moses.

[10] And there arose not a _____ since in Israel like unto _____ , whom the Lord knew _____ to _____ , [11] In all the _____ and the wonders, which the Lord sent him to do in the land of Egypt to Pharaoh, and to all his servants, and to all his land, [12] And in all that mighty _____ , and in all the great _____ which Moses shewed in the sight of all _____ .

Made in United States
Troutdale, OR
04/04/2024

18950296R10027